The
FUGITIVE SLAVE
RESCUE TRIAL
of
ROBERT MORRIS

Benjamin Robbins Curtis
on the Road to Dred Scott

The FUGITIVE SLAVE RESCUE TRIAL *of* ROBERT MORRIS

Benjamin Robbins Curtis *on the Road to* Dred Scott

JOHN D. GORDAN, III

TALBOT
PUBLISHING
Clark, New Jersey

ISBN 978-1-61619-392-8 (hardcover)
ISBN 978-1-61619-405-5 (paperback)

TALBOT PUBLISHING
AN IMPRINT OF
THE LAWBOOK EXCHANGE, LTD.
33 Terminal Avenue
Clark, New Jersey 07066-1321

*Please see our website for a selection of our other publications
and fine facsimile reprints of classic works of legal history:*
www.lawbookexchange.com

Library of Congress Cataloging-in-Publication Data

Gordan, John D., 1945- author.
 The fugitive slave rescue trial of Robert Morris : Benjamin Robbins Curtis on the road to Dred
Scott / by John D. Gordan, III.
    pages cm
 Includes bibliographical references and index.
 ISBN 978-1-61619-392-8 (hardcover : alk. paper) -- ISBN 1-61619-392-1 (hardcover : alk.
paper)
 1. Morris, Robert, 1823-1882--Trials, litigation, etc. 2. Trials (Political crimes and offenses)--
Massachusetts--History--19th century. 3. Minkins,
Shadrach--Trials, litigation, etc. 4. Curtis, Benjamin Robbins, 1809-1874 5. Fugitive slaves--
Legal status, laws, etc.--Massachusetts--History--19th
century. 6. Slavery--Law and legislation--United States--History--19th century. 7. Jury
nullification--United States--History--19th century. I. Title.
 KF223.M67 G67 2013
 342.7308'7--dc23

                                                            2013035139

Printed in the United States of America on acid-free paper

For Kitty Preyer,
Still loved, still mourned, by many.

ACKNOWLEDGMENTS

This small book performs a promise made to Kitty Preyer in 1989 to write about fugitive slave legal proceedings in Boston in the 1850s in which Richard Henry Dana, Jr., participated. As her essays — whether as they were published or as collected by her friends in *Blackstone in America: Selected Essays of Kathryn Preyer* (Cambridge 2009) — demonstrate, she was a brilliant and meticulous legal scholar and historian whose breadth of knowledge of early American history and whose ability to contextualize her particular topic in it were unrivaled. But even more than a scholar, she was a *teacher* who readily sacrificed her time for the success of her students, whether those formally enrolled in her classes at Wellesley College over the decades or merely those with shared interests whom she enrolled herself from the wider world of scholarship. Her generosity to her students was matchless — she was enthusiastic, encouraging, passionate, supportive, persistent — "And please don't leave Richard Henry Dana too far in the background" — and helpful to the point of providing material from her own library or ferreting it out elsewhere. She was a lighthearted, dignified, wonderful person whose cultivation was much wider than what she taught or wrote about– and brave.

This book would never have been written without the help and encouragement of Kitty Preyer's friend, R. Kent Newmyer. Author of the leading biographies of Chief Justice John Marshall and Justice Joseph Story, as well as a recent book on the trial of Aaron Burr, he selflessly read and commented on draft after draft, took my mind to places I never knew existed and urged me forward. Any insights in this book undoubtedly originated with him. I was also fortunate to have the benefit of comments on earlier drafts from my constant editor and friend, Conrad K. Harper, from another of Kitty Preyer's friends, Judge Morris Sheppard

Arnold, and from Professor David Konig of Washington University School of Law, a recognized expert in this area of American history.

Thanks are due also to the staff of the Boston Athenaeum, the American Antiquarian Society, the National Archives in Waltham, the Harvard Law School Library and the Massachusetts Historical Society for providing me with welcoming and ready access to the indispensable treasures in their custody and for giving me permission to include portions of them in the body of the book.

Finally, this book could never have been produced without the patient ministrations of my own Kitty, my wife of 46 years, and another friend of Kitty Preyer's, Valerie Horowitz of Talbot Publishing, and the support of Greg Talbot, the publisher.

TABLE OF CONTENTS

TABLE OF ILLUSTRATIONS

TABLE OF ABBREVIATIONS

Curtis Memoir — Benjamin R. Curtis, Jr. (ed.), *A Memoir of Benjamin Robbins Curtis with Some of His Professional and Miscellaneous Writings* (2 vols., Boston 1879)

Curtis Trial Notes — Benjamin Robbins Curtis, *Notes of cases before the Circuit Court 1851–1859* (11 vols.), Harvard Law School Library MS 4042, Vol. I

Curtis Constitutional History — George Ticknor Curtis, *Constitutional History of the United States from Their Declaration of Independence to the Close of Their Civil War* (2 vols., New York 1889 and 1896), Vol. II

Dana Journal — Robert F. Lucid (ed.), *The Journal of Richard Henry Dana, Jr.* (3 vols., Harvard 1968), Vol. II

Dana Papers — Richard Henry Dana, Jr. Legal Papers, 1844–1878, American Antiquarian Society, Worcester, Mass., Box 5, Files 1061 and 1062; Box 8, File 1271

Morris — *United States v. Morris, 26 F. Cas. 1323* (No. 15,815) (C.C.D.Mass 1851)

Parker Trial	Theodore Parker, *The Trial of Theodore Parker* (Boston 1855)
Story	William Wetmore Story (ed.), *Life and Letters of Joseph Story* (2 vols., Boston 1851)
Webster Papers	Charles M. Wiltse (ed.), *The Papers of Daniel Webster, Correspondence, Vol. 7, 1850–1852* (7 vols., 1975–1986, University Press of New England 1986)

INTRODUCTION

On February 15, 1851, maintaining the Boston tradition of liberating arrested slaves from the courtroom where their freedom was being adjudicated, a group of blacks forced their way into the federal courtroom, surrounded the slave as one of the deputy U.S. marshals shouted "shoot him, shoot him," and carried him out of the courthouse to freedom. Six trials of four of the alleged rescuers followed, with no convictions.

These Rescue prosecutions [1] are milestones, but not destinations, on roads elsewhere for both the participants and for legal historians. Shadrach, the rescued slave "otherwise called Frederic Minkins" according to the indictments, had already travelled from slavery in Norfolk, Virginia to permanent refuge in Canada.

Robert Morris, less than 30 years of age and the second black admitted to practice law in Massachusetts, was one of several abolitionist lawyers trying to save Shadrach from rendition to slavery in Virginia under the Fugitive Slave Act of 1850. His presence in the corridor outside the courtroom just before the rescue began and in the street as the crowd carried Shadrach away led to his indictment and two trials,

---

[1] The trials were held in Boston as follows:

5/28–6/6/1851	Scott	jury disagreed 6-6
6/6–6/17/1851	Hayden	jury voted 9-3 for conviction
6/17–6/18/1851	Morris	mistrial for juror antislavery bias
10/31–11/12/1851	Morris	acquittal
6/4–6/10/1852	Wright	jury voted 11-1 for conviction
10/22–10/27/52	Wright	acquittal

District Judge Peleg Sprague presided in the United States district court at the first three trials. Justice Benjamin Robbins Curtis, sitting in the United States circuit court, presided with Judge Sprague at Morris's second trial and sat alone at both of Wright's.

before his acquittal at the second opened the way for him to continue a career which was already successful after only four years at the Bar.[2]

For John Caphart, the slave catcher, the interrupted Shadrach rendition was a step on his path to immortalization as a dedicated, vicious sadist "without regard to sex or color" by United States Senator John Parker Hale, Harriet Beecher Stowe and even the House of Representatives of the Confederate States of America. For Richard Henry Dana, Jr., these prosecutions were an early opportunity to demonstrate, albeit as junior counsel for the defendants, the legal talent which would come into its own when, as United States district attorney for the district of Massachusetts during the Civil War, he was the prevailing counsel in the crucial 5–4 Supreme Court decision in *The Prize Cases* in 1863.

---

[2] Morris was the child of free blacks. Brought up in Salem, he became the household servant of John G. King, a prominent lawyer there. One of King's friends, the still more prominent Boston lawyer Ellis Gray Loring, employed Morris as a clerk in his office and mentored him to admission to the Bar. Stephen and Paul Kendrick, *Sarah's Long Walk* (Boston 2004); Stephen Kantrowitz, *More than Freedom: Fighting for Black Citizenship in a White Republic, 1829-1889* (New York 2012). In 1848 Morris filed the celebrated case of *Roberts v. Boston School Committee* and worked on its unsuccessful appeal. James Brewer Stewart, *Abolitionist Politics and the Coming of the Civil War* (U.Mass. 2008), 61–88. According to James Oliver Horton and Lois E. Horton, *Black Bostonians: Family Life and Community Struggle in the Antebellum North (rev. ed. New York 1999),* 60–61:

> Although Morris had also risen from humble roots, much of his life and all of his legal training had included the important influence of upper-class whites. His law practice was also partially dependent on white clients. Most of them were Irish, despite the notorious antipathy between blacks and Irish immigrants. Indeed, so many of his cases involved Irishmen that in some circles Morris was known as the "Irish lawyer."*** Many judges agreed that "by his tact and good nature he had won many cases where, if tried by almost any other attorney, the jury verdict would have been [the] reverse[]."

For Benjamin Robbins Curtis, presiding as Circuit Justice at trials held both after his recess appointment to the United States Supreme Court in September 1851 at the urging of Daniel Webster and after his confirmation in December of that year, the second *Morris* trial marked the beginning of a judicial tenure ending six years later with his dissent in *Dred Scott v. Sandford* and his resignation from the Court.[3] For his brother, George Ticknor Curtis, Justice Joseph Story's son-in-law and Daniel Webster's lawyer, this six-year period marked his passage from the Commissioner under the Fugitive Slave Act who issued the arrest warrant for Shadrach Minkins to one of the counsel for Dred Scott in the Supreme Court.

For legal historians these prosecutions typically make cameo appearances as part of a survey of the enforcement of the Fugitive Slave Act of 1850 or, more broadly, the evolution of the domestic law of slavery before the Civil War.[4] Today's scholars travel past the Rescue cases at such speed that they make elementary mistakes of fact or law. For example, Professor Maltz has Curtis presiding with District Judge Peleg Sprague in May and June 1851 at the acquittal of Robert Morris, when in actual fact Curtis (as Maltz notes in the preceding paragraph) was not given even his recess appointment until September 1851. The trials of James Scott, Lewis Hayden and Morris before Judge Sprague alone in May and June each ended in mistrials, and Morris's second trial, at which he was acquitted, was in November.

Similarly, Professor Lubet gives sole credit for the representation of Lewis Hayden, Robert Morris and Elizur Wright and for the acquittals of the latter two at their second trials to Richard Henry Dana, Jr., "who was then only thirty-six years old", never hinting that Dana, outstanding as he was, with only eleven years experience was lead counsel at none of the six trials: apart from Elizur Wright's first trial, where Wright defended without counsel, Dana was led in all of the

---

[3] 60 U.S. 393 (1857).
[4] The most recent of these are Steven Lubet, *Fugitive Justice–Runaways, Rescuers and Slavery on Trial* (Harvard 2010); Earl M. Maltz, *Slavery and the Supreme Court, 1825-1861* (Kansas 2009).

trials except the second trial of Wright by John Parker Hale, a much older and more experienced lawyer, appointed United States district attorney for the district of New Hampshire by President Andrew Jackson in 1834, and an abolitionist United States Senator from that state since 1847, and at the second trial of Wright by George F. Farley, more than twenty years Dana's senior at the Bar but frequently mischaracterized as his assistant.[5]

Indeed, even Hale's biographer asserts that "Hale had been present for only the first two trials," when in point of fact he was there not only for those but also for both Morris's first trial, immediately after Scott's and Hayden's, and for Morris's retrial in November, 1851.[6] His dedication was such that his absence from Wright's second trial was likely due only to his campaign for President of the United States as Free Soil Party candidate.

---

[5]Maltz, supra n. 4, at 186; Lubet, supra n. 4, at 141–145. In fairness, however, to Professors Maltz and Lubet, these errors of fact pale in comparison to those made by earlier historians. In the seminal and still unsurpassed *Justice Accused: Antislavery and the Judicial Process* (Yale 1975), 223n*, Robert M. Cover asserts that Charles G. Davis, another of Shadrach's abolitionist attorneys, was acquitted at a jury trial for aiding in Shadrach's rescue, when in fact at the preliminary hearing the commissioner found no probable cause to proceed further and discharged him; he was never indicted. In *From Abolition to Rights for All: The Making of a Reform Community in the Nineteenth Century* (U.Penn. 2008), 74, John T. Cumbler outdoes Cover in claiming: "Charles Davis came to trial first, before Benjamin Robbins Curtis, brother of George Ticknor Curtis, who issued the original warrant... and was found innocent." J. Clay Smith, Jr., *Emancipation: The Making of the Black Lawyer 1844–1944* (UPenn. 1993), 98–99, asserts that all the defendants were convicted after trials before a United States commissioner but that those convictions were set aside on technical grounds on appeal to the United States Circuit Court of Appeals, and Morris was later acquitted after remand for a new trial in the District Court; however, Dean Smith does note that Morris thanked both Hale and Dana for their defense of the accused. *Id.* at 117 n. 40.

[6] Richard H. Sewell, *John P. Hale and the Politics of Abolition* (Harvard 1965), 142.

Similarly, in the recent biography of Justice Curtis, his opinion in *United States v. Robert Morris,* wrongly denying the historic legitimacy of juries as judges of the law at the second *Morris* trial,[7] the first of the Rescue trials at which he presided, is whitewashed as illustrative of his fidelity to "the principle of uniformity and the rule of law." [8] Perhaps projecting the attitude of his *Dred Scott* dissent six years later to this earlier date, Justice Curtis's biographer offers a brief, one-sided apology for the ruling, which was in any event just one of his three opinions in *Morris.*[9]

Fortunately for those interested in the Rescue cases, there are two excellent treatments, both by the late Professor Gary Collison,[10] whose focus was limited to them and who was as careful as he was thorough in his research and treatment of the facts. But, like the authors of other book-length presentations of individual fugitive slave cases,[11] Collison was a professor of English, not a lawyer, and understandably avoids an in-depth analysis of Justice Curtis's reported rulings at the second *Morris* trial.

These trials demand study because of the distortions of fact, of law and of the judicial process which either occurred at them or have since been created by historians' errors and

---

[7] *United States v. Morris*, 26 F. Cas. 1323, 1331–1336 (No. 15,815) (C.C.D.Mass.1851).

[8] Stuart Streichler, *Justice Curtis in the Civil War Era: At the Crossroads of American Constitutionalism* (Virginia 2005), 59.

[9] See *Morris* at 1324 and 1329.

[10] *Shadrach Minkins: From Fugitive Slave to Citizen* (Harvard 1997); "'This Flagitious Offense': Daniel Webster and the Shadrach Rescue Cases," *New England Quarterly* (December 1995), Vol. 68, 609–625. The article, although far more limited in scope than the book, actually provides the most detailed, accurate and focused factual analysis available of the Rescue trials.

[11] E.G., Albert J. Von Frank, *The Trials of Anthony Burns: Freedom and Slavery in Emerson's Boston* (Harvard 1998); Steven Weisenburger, *Modern Medea: A Family Story of Slavery and Child-Murder from the Old South* (New York 1998). H. Robert Baker's excellent *The Rescue of Joshua Glover: A Fugitive Slave, The Constitution and the Coming of the Civil War* (Ohio 2006), is the work of a history professor.

revisionism, so extensive that a single book can focus fully only on one, here the trial of Robert Morris.

First, although in its origin this book was intended to be a paean to Richard Henry Dana, Jr., an energetic and committed abolitionist lawyer, research proved that Dana did not have the first chair in *Morris* or any of the other Rescue trials, and his role in these trials was eclipsed both by the lead counsel, John Parker Hale, who proves to be the forgotten hero of this story, and by the presiding Justice.

Second, some historians have breezily suggested that Morris was obviously guilty and his defense therefore perjured, but the evidence recorded in Dana's still extant case files, Justice Curtis's comprehensive trial notes at Harvard Law School and detailed reports in *The Commonwealth* is far more equivocal than that.

Third, doubtless because of his dissent in *Dred Scott*, because of Dana's praise in passing, in his diary at the time and in his eulogy of Curtis years later, for the impartiality of Justice Curtis's jury charge in *Morris*, and perhaps because his rulings at the *Morris* trial have not been analyzed in context, no one has recognized that Justice Curtis, entirely predictably but in a subtle and artful way, in his legal rulings and jury instructions repeatedly put his thumb hard on the scale against Morris, distorting existing law to do it, in one instance with lasting effect.

Fourth, while Justice Curtis's subsequent jury charge at the second trial of Elizur Wright in October 1852 seems to reflect some softening of his partisan rulings in *Morris*, his dismissal of the indictments in the parallel case of *United States v. Stowell*—arising from the failed rescue of another fugitive slave, Anthony Burns, in 1854—and his dissent in *Dred Scott* are fully consistent with the legal and political imperatives he expressed in 1850, not long before his appointment to the Supreme Court:

> There are many political principles with which our people are well acquainted, and there is an intuitive disposition to obey the law very prevalent among them; but that the Constitution of the United States is a *law*, —binding by

each clause the conduct of every man in the country in the particular to which such clause relates, equally obligatory whether obeyed or disobeyed, —that organized disobedience is rebellion, and, if force is used, insurrection or revolution, according to the event, —are things which a great many teachers of political morals, of the present day, do not seem to have taken into their minds at all.

I blame no one for arriving at the opinion, either by reasoning or impulse, that fugitive slaves ought not to be restored to their masters. But having arrived at this opinion, there remains another step; and I wish these Unitarian clergymen would sit down calmly and measure, or attempt to measure, its length, and look as steadily as they can, for one moment at least, into the place where that step must carry us.

I want to see somebody come manfully up to the point, and attempt to show that the moral duty which we owe to the fugitive slave, when in conflict with the moral duty we owe to our country and its laws, is so plainly superior thereto, that we may and ought to engage in a revolution on account of it. I should be glad to see this attempted, because it presents the true issue, and I am sure the attempt must fail. Wendell Phillips and his followers have taken the only sound ground; and their success in maintaining it does not seem to be very encouraging to others to join them there.... [12]

---

[12] Benjamin R. Curtis, Jr. (ed.), *A Memoir of Benjamin Robbins Curtis with Some of His Professional and Miscellaneous Writings* (2 vols., Boston 1879) (hereafter "Curtis Memoir"), Vol. 1, 122.

Robert Morris
Courtesy of the Social Law Library, Boston

CHAPTER I

The Historical Context

In 1829 Benjamin Robbins Curtis started as a student at Harvard Law School in the first class taught by Joseph Story; his younger brother, George Ticknor Curtis, followed him there four years later. Story thought highly of Benjamin Robbins Curtis as a law student and told him so in later years:

> I will not disguise that I have the greatest pride in you as one of my law pupils; and I trust that, even if a solitary lesson at the School has left any deep impression on your memory, it is no less a consolation to the Professor who still survives, that his own recollections of your devotion to the law while here gave him the strongest assurances of your future eminence.[1]

"Devotion to the law" is the core of Curtis's statement quoted above, and in the sense Story meant it as something that he and Curtis clearly shared. Story by that time had already faced the very issue Curtis raised in the fugitive slave context and had resolved it the way Curtis thought it should be; it was likely Story's teaching and example that inspired what Curtis wrote five years after Story's death in 1845.

Joseph Story's service as Dane Professor of Law at Harvard until his death in the fall of 1845, and from 1811 as a justice of the Supreme Court, sitting with his brethren in Washington and, as circuit justice, with the district judges in New England, was hardly enough to keep him fully occupied.

---

[1] *Ibid.*, at 102–103. Letter of Joseph Story to Benjamin Robbins Curtis dated January 2, 1844.

He also wrote and published numerous full-length learned treatises on various aspects of law. Behind the scenes he was a tireless drafter of federal legislation, either because he saw the need of it or by particular request, often from Daniel Webster, with whom he had the closest personal and political ties.[2] The Storys and the Websters traveled together recreationally to Niagara Falls for weeks in the summer of 1825.[3] Story thought highly of Webster from early days, writing after the

---

[2] See, *e.g.*, William Wetmore Story (ed.), *Life and Letters of Joseph Story* (2 vols. Boston 1851): Vol. 1, 435–441: Story to Webster, January 4, 1824 (Story proposes to update his 1818 draft of a federal crimes bill, which is passed in 1825; also says: "What hope of a Bankrupt Act? Why, will you not ask me to put one into the shape of a code in articles? I want to try my hand at codifying a Bankrupt ordinance."); Story to Webster, January 10, 1824 (adding justices to the Supreme Court or creating a circuit system). See also Fletcher Webster (ed.), *The Private Correspondence of Daniel Webster* (2 Vols. Boston 1857), Vol. 1, 348–349: Webster to Story, April 10, 1824: "I shall call up some bills reported by our committee, as soon as possible. The gentlemen of the West will propose a clause, requiring the assent of a majority of all the judges to a judgment, which pronounces a state law void, as being in violation of the constitution or laws of the United States. Do you see any great evil in such a provision? *** In what phraseology would you make such a provision? As to the bankrupt law, pray give me your ideas of an outline…;" 412: Webster to Story, December 26, 1826: "You will have seen in a late National Intelligencer, the report of last year, respecting the courts. Something undoubtedly will be done on that subject this session. What shall we do? Shall we increase your bench by two? Shall we relieve your bench of all circuit duties, and establish a uniform system of circuit courts?" Story, supra, Vol. 2, 330: Story to Webster, May 10, 1840, responding at length to Webster's request for advice regarding the proposed bankruptcy act.

So close were they professionally that Webster had no hesitancy in providing Story with privately printed copies of his argument in the *Dartmouth College Case* while it was sub judice to lobby more hesitant justices with. Webster, supra, Vol. 1 at 287 (Webster to Story, September 9, 1818: "…you will of course do it in the manner least likely to lead to a feeling that any indecorum has been committed by the plaintiffs.").

[3] Story, Vol. 1, 449–480, 487.

1820 Massachusetts constitutional convention arising from the separation of its Maine territory:

> Our friend Webster has gained a noble reputation. He was before known as a lawyer; but he has now secured the title of an eminent and enlightened statesman. It was a glorious field for him, and he has had an ample harvest. The whole force of his great mind was brought out, and in several speeches he commanded universal admiration. He always led the van, and was most skillful and instantaneous in attack and retreat. He fought, as I have told him, in the "imminent deadly breach;" and all I could do was to skirmish in aid of him upon some of the enemy's outposts. On the whole, I never was more proud of any display of his in my life, and I am much deceived, if the well-earned popularity so justly and so boldly acquired by him on this occasion, does not carry him, if he lives, to the Presidency.[4]

Early in his lengthy tenure on the Supreme Court, Story's statements as a single justice on circuit had made clear his abhorrence of slavery, well beyond the international slave trade which was the immediate context for his remarks.[5] Ironically, one of these statements:

> The existence of Slavery under any shape is so repugnant to the natural rights of man and the dictates of justice, that it seems difficult to find for it any adequate justification. *** It is to be lamented indeed, that slavery exists in any part of our country; but it should be considered that it is not an evil introduced in the present age. It has been entailed upon a part of the country by their ancestors...

was made to the Grand Jury in Portland, Maine, soon after Maine's admission as a state as part of the Missouri Compromise in 1820, which Story opposed vehemently

---

[4] Story, Vol. 1, 394–396 (Story to Jeremiah Mason, January 21, 1821).
[5] *A Charge Delivered to the Grand Juries of the Circuit Court, at the October Term, 1819, in Boston, and at the November Term, 1819, in Providence, and Published at their Unanimous Request;* Cover, *supra,* page xvii, n. 5, 238–243.

because it included the extension of domestic slavery by the admission of Missouri as a slave state.[6] A year and a half later, a case involving a French slave ship seized off the coast of Africa led to another passionate denunciation of slavery by Story, who held that the international slave trade violated the law of nations, expressly refusing to follow a contrary decision by Sir William Scott of the High Court of Admiralty, whom Story greatly admired.[7]

At about the same time Story shared with Daniel Webster his willingness to provide personal financial support to colonization, in the hope that it would lead to emancipation:

> My own faith in the practicability of the scheme has never been strong, and I have never affected to disguise it. Still, however, I am ready to accede to any plan to give it a fair chance of success. For, I agree with you in thinking that we ought not to despair, when such men as Judge Washington and Mr. Key are so deeply and earnestly in the belief of its success.

> I am ready to subscribe as a donor to the extent of what I think is my reasonable share.*** I believe the Colonization Society has now one good effect, and that is to nourish a strong distaste for slavery among the most kind and benevolent of the Southern States; and it gives countenance

---

[6] *Charge Delivered to the Grand Jury of the Circuit Court of the United States, at its First Session in Portland for the Judicial District of Maine, May 8, 1820* (Portland 1820), 13-14. Story, supra n. 13, Vol. 1, 359–369 (referring to his "rooted aversion to slavery in Missouri and in Africa); Robert Ernst, *Rufus King: American Federalist* (UNC 1968), 371–372 (King had his speeches in the Senate against the expansion of slavery into Missouri printed as a pamphlet which "Webster, Gore and Justice Joseph Story used...to whip up opinion in Boston."); R. Kent Newmyer, *Supreme Court Justice Joseph Story: Statesman of the Old Republic* (UNC 1985), 166.

[7] *United States v. The La Jeune Eugenie*, 26 F. Cas. 832 (No. 15,551) (C.C.D. Mass. 182[1]). Sadly, when the same issue reached the Supreme Court in *The Antelope*, 23 U.S. 66, 117–123 (1825), Story kept silent as Chief Justice Marshall ruled the opposite way.

Carte-de-visite, Joseph Story, Mathew Brady & Studio
Courtesy of Special Collections, Fine Arts Library, Harvard University

to them in cherishing a public enthusiasm in favor of the ultimate emancipation of slaves. I think I have perceived a growing feeling of the injustice of slavery among all those who have been ardently attached to its objects. This is no inconsiderable gain.[8]

---

[8] Story, Vol. 1, 421 (Story to Webster, August 6, 1822). However, Story was not always so charitable about the southern states. In the first edition of his landmark *Commentaries on the Constitution of the United States* (3 vols., Boston 1833), Vol. 3, Section 1805, he explained the

But, as expressed in his *Commentaries* a decade earlier, Story had no doubt of the Constitutional grant of protection to Southern slaveholders in the provision for the recovery of domestic fugitive slaves and that the duty of the Supreme Court was to uphold the Fugitive Slave Act of 1793 as the mechanism for its enforcement and an adjunct to lawful slaveholder self-help.[9] Speaking for a plurality of the Court, Story used *Prigg* as an opportunity to federalize the rendition of fugitive slaves and to exclude the states from participation in it, over the dissent of Chief Justice Taney and others who argued that the states had a duty to support fugitive slave renditions also. Not only are the implications, intended or otherwise, of *Prigg* the subject of intensifying current scholarly debate,[10] they were clouded in ambiguity almost

---

origins of the fugitive slave provision in Article IV of the Constitution thus:

> The clause was introduced into the constitution solely for the benefit of the slave-holding states, to enable them to reclaim their fugitive slaves, who should have escaped into other states, where slavery was not tolerated. The want of such a provision under the confederation was felt, as a grievous inconvenience by the slave-holding states, since in many states no aid whatsoever would be allowed to the owners; and sometimes indeed they met with open resistance. In fact, it cannot escape the attention of every intelligent reader, that many sacrifices of opinion and feeling are to be found made by the Eastern and Middle states to the peculiar interests of the south. This forms no just subject of complaint; but it should for ever repress the delusive and mischievous notion, that the south has not at all time had its full share of benefits from the Union.

[9] *Prigg v. Pennsylvania*, 41 U.S. 539 (March 1, 1842). The case involved Pennsylvania's effort to punish slavecatchers from Maryland who had come into Pennsylvania to seize a slave from Maryland, Margaret Morgan, residing there with her Pennsylvania-born children. Unable to secure cooperation from a Pennsylvania justice of the peace to authorize a legal rendition, they seized her and her children and took them back to Maryland.
[10] See, e.g., H. Robert Baker, *Prigg v. Pennsylvania: Slavery, the Supreme Court, and the Ambivalent Constitution* (Kansas 2012); *ibid.*, "The Fugitive Slave Clause and the Antebellum Constitution", *Law and History Review* (2012), Vol. 30, 1133. Leslie Friedman Goldstein, "A

from the start, in part by Story himself and not long afterwards by his son.

William Wetmore Story noted that *Prigg* "conforms to those principles of interpretation in favor of the Federal Government...that the Constitution creates, not a mere confederation of States, but a government of the people, endowed with all powers appropriate or incidental to carry out its provisions..." He also repeatedly contended that his father rightly claimed *Prigg* as a "triumph of freedom" because its exclusion of state authorities from the rendition process in favor of the occasional federal judge in any state made "the Act of 1793 a dead letter in the free States." [11]

Information which William Wetmore Story omitted from his book creates a different impression. Daniel Webster was not the only legislator Story counseled: in 1842 another was Senator John M. Berrien of Georgia, chairman of the Senate Judiciary Committee. On February 8 and April 29, 1842, both before and after the *Prigg* decision, Justice Story wrote to Berrien with legislative proposals. William Wetmore Story reproduces these letters but introduces ellipses into the second.[12] The portion omitted was identified and published in substantial part for the first time in 1971, 120 years after William Wetmore Story excised it:

> In the MSS Bill, which I handed you, the provision was *general*, that in *all cases*, where by the Laws of U. States, powers were conferred on State Magistrates, the same powers might be exercised by Commissioners appointed by the Circuit Courts. I was induced to make the provision thus general, because State Magistrates now generally refuse to act, & cannot be compelled to act; and the Act of 1793 respecting fugitive slaves confers the power on States Magistrates to act in delivering up Slaves. You saw, in the case of Prigg... how the duty was evaded, or declined. In

---

Triumph of Freedom After All? Prigg v. Pennsylvania Re-examined," *Law and History Review* (2011), Vol. 29, 763.

[11] Story, Vol. 2, 392–398.

[12] Story, Vol. 2, 402–405. A third letter, dated July 23, 1842, is also reproduced. *Ibid.* at 405–406.

conversing with several of my Brethren on the Supreme
Court, we all thought that it would be a great improvement,
& would tend much to facilitate the recapture of Slaves, if
Commissioners of the Circuit Court were clothed with like
powers. This might be done without creating the slightest
sensation in Congress, if the provisions were made
general... It would then pass without observation. The
Courts would appoint commissioners in every county, &
thus meet the practical difficulty now presented by the
refusal of State Magistrates. It might be unwise to provoke
debate to insert a Special clause in the first section,
referring to the fugitive Slave Act of 1793. Suppose you
add at the end of the first section: '& shall & may exercise
all the powers, that any State judge, Magistrate, or Justice
of the Peace may exercise under any other Law or Laws of
the United States.'[13]

Story's biographer distinguishes "the antislavery position
(which Story held) from abolitionism (which he condemned
with a passion...)."[14]

Even without knowledge of Justice Story's behind-the-
scenes efforts to undo the "triumph of freedom," the
abolitionists cheerfully damned him because *Prigg* nullified
state personal liberty laws. In his newspaper, *The Liberator*,
William Lloyd Garrison wrote that the *Prigg* decision, among
other things:

is to be spit upon, hooted at, trampled in the dust, resolutely
and openly, at all hazards, by every one who claims to be a
man, and in whose bosom remains a spark of the fire of
liberty. The people of Massachusetts will scorn to regard it.
The soil of Massachusetts will be consecrated ground, and
the victim of oppression who flies to it for
shelter...SHALL BE FREE.[15]

---

[13] James McClellan, *Joseph Story and the American Constitution*
(Oklahoma 1971), 262–263 n. 94.
[14] Newmyer, *supra*, page 4, n.6, at 351.
[15] Wendell P. Garrison and Francis J. Garrison, *William Lloyd Garrison
1805–1879: The Story of His Life Told by his Children* (4 vols. New
York 1889), Vol. 3, 59 n.1.

Just a few weeks later Garrison's assertion would be put to the test when, in the first fugitive slave apprehension in Boston in some years,[16] George Latimer was arrested under the Fugitive Slave Act of 1793 on a warrant issued on October 22, 1842 by Justice Story himself. A hearing before Justice Story was scheduled in the warrant for November 5; in the meantime Latimer was remanded to the custody of his claimant. Attempts to obtain Latimer's release by forcible rescue and, subsequently, *habeas corpus* from Chief Justice Shaw failed. Pressure on the Boston jailor to release Latimer from the custody arranged privately by Latimer's owner led to Latimer's sale to a group of Bostonians, who liberated him.[17]

Latimer's liberation was preceded by a meeting of abolitionists at Faneuil Hall on October 30, at which Justice Story was christened "Slave-Catcher-In-Chief for the New England States."[18] One of the speakers was Wendell Phillips, who in addition to announcing that "my *curse* be on the Constitution of the United States," proclaimed that "any judge who should grant a certificate" of rendition under the Act of 1793 "would be the basest of all: 'And in the lowest deep, a

---

[16] In an early case in 1836, two black women sailed into Boston and were confronted by a person, claiming to be the agent of their owner, who persuaded the captain of the vessel to detain them despite the documents they carried establishing their freedom. An application for *habeas corpus* was made to Chief Justice Lemuel Shaw on August 1, with the women present in the courtroom; he ruled that the captain had no authority to detain the women under the Fugitive Slave Act and ordered them discharged. When the agent made a statement about obtaining a warrant for them, the spectators rushed forward and swept the women away and out of the courthouse, despite Chief Justice Shaw's demand for order and his personal efforts to keep the courtroom door shut. Leonard W. Levy, "The 'Abolition Riot': Boston's First Slave Rescue," *New England Quarterly* (1952), Vol. 25, 85.

[17] Paul Finkelman, *Slavery in the Courtroom* (Washington, D.C. 1985), 64-65. The affirmance of the convictions of participants in the effort to rescue Latimer is reported as *Commonwealth v. Tracy,* 46 Mass. (5 Metcalf) 536 (1843).

[18] "The Latimer Case," *The Monthly Law Reporter* (1843), Vol. V, 481, 486.

lower deep, still threatening to devour him, opens wide." [19] The judge in that position was, of course, Joseph Story, and Wendell Phillips had been one of his students at Harvard Law School, graduating in 1833, between the two Curtis brothers.

Fugitive slave cases in Massachusetts split Justice Story's alumni into two camps. The two Curtis brothers and Charles Devens, the United States marshal in Boston and later Attorney General of the United States, were Webster Whigs. In the abolitionist camp were Phillips; Richard Henry Dana, Jr., who graduated in 1840, and would later be counsel in fugitive slave cases; Charles Sumner, who graduated in 1834, was Story's favorite pupil, reporter of his decisions, for a time his intended successor as Dane Professor, and ultimately assault victim while serving as United States Senator;[20] and Charles G. Davis, one of Shadrach's counsel at his abortive rendition hearing and one of the many arrested in the aftermath of his rescue.

In a category by himself is Justice Story's son, William Wetmore Story, who obtained his degree in 1841 but only practiced briefly, and who claimed that *Prigg* made the Fugitive Slave Act of 1793 a "dead letter in the free States", despite his father's subsequent warrant for George Latimer's arrest under it. In his 1851 two-volume biography of his father, William Wetmore Story mentioned Latimer only when asserting that *Prigg* sparked the state penal statute prohibiting the unofficial custodial arrangement for Latimer, leading to his availability for purchase. In doing so, despite his suppression of the 1842 correspondence with Senator Berrien, Story actually claimed for his father credit for the enactment of the Fugitive Slave Act of 1850: "Such, indeed, was the difficulty of reclaiming a fugitive slave after this decision, that Congress, by the stringent Act of 1850 now in force,

---

[19] Lorenzo Sears, *Wendell Phillips: Orator and Agitator* (New York 1909), 102.

[20] On May 21, 1856, while seated at his desk on the Senate floor, Sumner was beaten into unconsciousness with a cane wielded by South Carolina Congressman Preston Brooks. David Herbert Donald, *Charles Sumner and the Coming of the Civil War* (New York 1960), 241–260.

considered it necessary to revise the legislation on this subject."[21]

Justice Story responded to the abolitionists in kind. Future President Rutherford B. Hayes, who graduated from Harvard Law School in 1845, records in his journal the following lecture by Justice Story in December 1843 "on the duty of American citizens to adhere honestly and implicitly to the Constitution":

> There is a clause in the Constitution which gives to the slaveholders the right of reclaiming a fugitive slave from the free States. This clause some people wish to evade, or are willing wholly to disregard. If one part of the country can disregard one part of the Constitution, another section may refuse to obey that part which seems to bear hard upon its interests, and thus the Union will become a 'mere rope of sand'; and the Constitution, worse than a dead letter, an apple of discord in our midst, a fruitful source of reproach, bitterness, and hatred, and in the end discord and civil war.... *** Such must inevitably follow the first success of those mad men, who even now are ready to stand up in public assemblies, and in the name of conscience, liberty, or the rights of man, to boast that they are willing and ready to bid farewell to that Constitution under which we have lived and prospered for more than half a century, and which I trust may be transmitted, unimpaired, from generation to generation for many centuries to come. It was the result of compromise and a spirit of concession and forbearance, and will end when that spirit dies in the hearts of this people. Let no man think to excuse himself from any duty which it enjoins. ***[22]

Benjamin Robbins Curtis had learned his lessons well.

---

[21] Story, Vol. 2, 394.

[22] Charles Richard Williams, *The Life of Rutherford Birchard Hayes: Nineteenth President of the United States* (2 vols. Boston 1914), Vol. 1, 36–37.

'CONQUERING PREJUDICE,'
or
"Fulfilling a Constitutional duty with alacrity."

"My God! —My child! — Will no one help! — Is there no mercy!"

"Any man can perform an agreeable duty — it is not every one that can perform a disagreeable duty."

"By heaven! he exceeds my most sanguine expectation — he marks his way so clearly & treads so loyally on the track of the Constitution. — It is more than great — it is sublime. — I feel a great sense of relief."

Peter Kramer, "Conquering Prejudice," lithograph
Worcester Art Museum, Worcester, Massachusetts,
Charles E. Goodspeed Collection, 1910. 48.3374

CHAPTER II

The Fugitive Slave Act of 1850

The next significant judicial proceeding involving fugitive slaves in Boston was in February 1851, nearly six years after Justice Story's death, with the arrest — and later rescue — of Shadrach Minkins under the new Fugitive Slave Act of 1850, enacted as part of the Compromise of 1850. That act was very much the product of the famous speech Daniel Webster made in the Senate on March 7, 1850, supporting Southern interests in the midst of the dispute over slavery in the territories between the Northern and Southern States.[1]

A speech by Ralph Waldo Emerson demonstrates that Webster was an individual of extraordinary presence and intellect. But Emerson also described Webster's influence in connection with the Fugitive Slave Act in 1850:

> Now I have lived all my life without suffering any known inconvenience from American slavery. I never saw it; never heard the whip; I never felt the check on my free speech and action; until the other day when Webster by his personal influence brought the Fugitive Slave Law on the country. I say Mr. Webster, for though the bill was not his, yet it is notorious that he was the life and soul of it, that he gave all he had, it cost him his life. And under the shadow of his great name, inferior men sheltered themselves and threw their ballots for it, and made the law. I say inferior men; they were all sorts of what are called brilliant men, accomplished men, men of high office, a President of the United States, senators, and of eloquent speech, but men without self-respect, without character, and it was droll to

---

[1] Robert Remini, *Daniel Webster: The Man and His Time* (New York 1997), 662–681.

see that office, age, fame, talent, even a repute for honesty, all count for nothing. They had no opinions, they had no memory for what they had been saying like the Lord's prayer, all in their lifetime; they were only looking to what their great captain did, and if he jumped, they jumped, — if he stood on his head, they did.[2]

Webster returned to Boston in late April, 1850, to be greeted outside of his hotel by a large crowd and welcomed in an address given by Benjamin Robbins Curtis, by then an accomplished lawyer and minor political figure, who praised him for "the ability and fidelity which you have brought to the defense of the Constitution and Union of these United States." In reply, referring to "topics in regard to some of which there exist both misstatements and misapprehension...the greatest...the question respecting the delivery of fugitives from service," Webster said:

But, Mr. Curtis, and gentlemen, there are in regard to that topic duties absolutely incumbent on the Commonwealth, — duties imposed by the Constitution, — absolutely incumbent on every person who holds office in Massachusetts under her own constitution and laws, or under those of the nation. She is bound, and those persons are bound, to the discharge of a duty, — of a disagreeable duty. We call upon her to discharge that duty as an affair of high morals and high political principles.[3]

Webster's relationship to Benjamin Robbins Curtis, prior to any evidence that he was a candidate for a position on the

---

[2] Ralph Waldo Emerson, "The Fugitive Slave Law" in (L. Gougeon and J. Myerson, eds.), *Emerson's Antislavery Writings* (Yale 1995), 73, 74–76.
[3] Curtis Memoir, Vol. I, 115–120. The Curtis family were close political allies of Webster's; Benjamin's younger brother, George Ticknor Curtis, was Webster's personal lawyer and with him just before his death in 1852. He and his uncle, George Ticknor, hosted Webster on his last trip to Boston before he died. Charles M. Wiltse (ed.), *The Papers of Daniel Webster, Correspondence, Vol. 7, 1850–1852* (Univ. Press of New England 1986) 355 n.1 (hereafter "Webster Papers".) See also Von Frank, *supra*, page xvii, n.11, at 114–117.

Supreme Court, may have been as Emerson described. Certainly Curtis's public activities as an adherent to Webster's position on slavery in 1850, described above, reflect that. But there also appears to have been a bond of admiration, almost an emotional one, between Curtis and Webster, reflected in the conclusion of a letter Curtis wrote to Webster thanking him for a copy of speech Webster had made in July 1850, to which Curtis had made some contribution:

> I am not given to professions, but I can say with truth, & it gratifies me to say it, that your relation to the great interests of the country has been, & is such, that I should suspect my own patriotism, if I were not disposed to serve you when I can.[4]

The "disagreeable duty" became federal law when President Millard Fillmore signed the Fugitive Slave Act on September 18, 1850, establishing a network of commissioners appointed by the circuit courts to conduct summary rendition proceedings, much like the one that Justice Story had proposed to Senator Berrien eight years earlier. Daniel Webster was the new Secretary of State and as such responsible for federal law enforcement.[5] In response, Boston's blacks met on September 30, elected Lewis Hayden president of the meeting and Robert Morris head of a committee to address the threat of enforcement. On October 14, an abolitionist meeting was held in Faneuil Hall, chaired by Charles Francis Adams, son and grandson of Presidents of the United States, and addressed by Adams, Wendell Phillips, Richard Henry Dana, Jr., and Frederick Douglass. The Vigilance Committee, which had dissolved after the *Latimer* case, was reconstituted with Hayden, Morris, Dana and Parker among its leaders. In November the Committee, through a combination of political pressure tactics and publicly hounding the slave catchers in pursuit of William and Ellen

---

[4] Letter dated August 21, 1850, Curtis Papers, Library of Congress.

[5] The Attorney General's control of United States district attorneys began in 1861 (12 Stat. 285) and was completed with the establishment of the Justice Department in 1870 (16 Stat. 132).

Lewis Hayden
Courtesy of the Boston Athanaeum

Craft, fugitive slaves living in Boston, succeeded in protecting the Crafts and spiriting them out of town.[6]

Webster, assisted by Benjamin Robbins Curtis, was active in trying to get the Fugitive Slave Act enforced in Boston. Webster had passed through Boston in early November trying unsuccessfully to spur the apprehension of the Crafts.[7] To that end, on November 9, Curtis provided the United States marshal with an opinion in favor of the constitutionality of the new Fugitive Slave Act.[8]

---

[6] Collison, *Shadrach Minkins, supra*, page xvii, n. 10, 75–100.
[7] Webster Papers 177–178, 180–181.
[8] A substantial portion of the opinion — which was printed in full in the *Boston Daily Advertiser* on November 19, 1850 and is reproduced in part

On November 26, with Webster's support, a Union meeting of Webster Whigs was held at Faneuil Hall, the speakers arranged for by Benjamin's brother George Ticknor Curtis, a commissioner appointed under the Fugitive Slave Act to adjudicate the removal of fugitive slaves reclaimed by their owners. Thomas P. Curtis, a distant cousin of George T. and Benjamin Robbins Curtis and uncle of the latter's wife, presided at the meeting.[9] At Webster's suggestion, one of the speakers was Benjamin Robbins Curtis, who made short work of fugitive slaves, calling them "foreigners": "With the rights of these persons I firmly believe Massachusetts has nothing to do. It is enough for us that they have no right to be here."

Curtis also attacked the Rev. Theodore Parker, the religious leader of the abolitionists and a future defendant in the United States circuit court in a prosecution in 1855 before Justice Curtis growing out the attempted rescue of Anthony Burns in May 1854. What Curtis said on that occasion emphatically drew the battle lines for the jury nullification issue that would be fought out a year later in the United States circuit court at the trial of Robert Morris between Curtis, presiding under a recess appointment as a justice of the Supreme Court of the United States, and Morris's lawyers, John Parker Hale and Richard Henry Dana, Jr.:

> There has been heard within these walls, addressed to a public meeting, and received with approbation at that meeting, the declaration that an article of the Constitution of the United States shall not be executed, *law or no law*. A

---

in John Codman Hurd, *The Law of Freedom and Bondage in the United States* (2 vols. Boston 1862), Vol. II, 678–680 — addresses whether "judicial inquiries, summarily made, designed to accomplish some limited and special object, but not to try and finally settle the right in contestation" could be conducted by commissioners, rather than Article III judges. Curtis concluded that such a "summary inquiry" is not "a case arising under the laws of the United States" for Article III purposes. William Wetmore Story, struggling with *Prigg*, misconstrues his father's opinion otherwise. Story, Vol. 2, 396. Webster praised Curtis's opinion to the President. Webster Papers at 232.

[9] *Id.* at 178–179; Collison, *Shadrach Minkins, supra,* page xvii, n. 10, 102. Von Frank, *supra,* page xvii, n. 11, 117.

gentleman offered a resolve, which passed at a public meeting *here,* that "Constitution or no Constitution, law or no law, we will not allow a fugitive slave to be taken from Massachusetts." *** The chairman of a public meeting declared *here* that "the law will be resisted, and if the fugitive resists, and if he slay the slavehunter, or even the Marshal, and if he therefore be brought before a jury of Massachusetts men, that jury will not convict him." *** The chairman of a public meeting here has ventured to assure such persons that judges and jurors will violate their oaths to protect them from punishment; and as if there should be nothing wanting to exhibit the madness which has possessed men's minds, murder and perjury have been erected into virtues, and in this city preached from the sacred desk. I must not be suspected of exaggerating in the least degree. I read, therefore, the following passage from a sermon preached and published in this city: —

Let me suppose a case which may happen here, and before long. A woman flies from South Carolina to Massachusetts to escape from bondage. Mr. Greatheart aids her in her escape, harbors and conceals her, and is brought to trial for it. The punishment is a fine of one thousand dollars and imprisonment for six months. I am drawn to serve as a juror and pass upon this offence. I may refuse to serve and be punished for that, leaving men with no scruples to take my place, or I may take the juror's oath to give a verdict according to the law and the testimony. The law is plain, let us suppose, and the testimony conclusive. Greatheart himself confesses that he did the deed alleged, saving one ready to perish. The judge charges that, if the jurors are satisfied of that fact, then they must return that he is guilty. This is a nice matter. Here are two questions. The one put to me in my official capacity as a juror is this, — "Did Greatheart aid the woman?" The other, put to me in my natural character as a man, is this, — "Will you help to punish Greatheart with fine and imprisonment for helping a woman to obtain her inalienable rights?" If I have extinguished my manhood by my juror's oath, then I shall do my official business and find Greatheart guilty, and I shall seem to be a true man; but if I value my manhood, I shall answer after my natural duty to love a man and not hate him, to do him justice, not injustice, to allow him the natural rights he has not alienated, and shall say "Not guilty." Then men will call me forsworn and a liar, but I think human nature will justify the verdict...

The man who attacks me to reduce me to slavery, in that moment alienates his right to life, and if I were the fugitive, and could escape in no other way, I would kill him with as little compunction as I would drive a mosquito from my face.

I should like to ask the reverend preacher, when he goes into court, and holds up his hand, and calls on his Maker to attest to the sincerity of his vow to render a true verdict according to the law and the evidence, whether he does *that* as a man, or in some other capacity? And I should also like to ask him, in what capacity he expects to receive the punishment which would await him here and hereafter, if he were to do what he recommends to others.[10]

The "reverend preacher," Theodore Parker, proved to be in the audience and offered in vain to answer the questions Curtis undoubtedly had intended rhetorically.[11]

Although, for reasons that do not appear, Hale waited until the second *Morris* trial to raise this issue in the Rescue cases, he had long since staked out the contrary position. In January 1842, Hale, then recently ousted by President Tyler as United States district attorney for New Hampshire, had insisted on the right of the jury to determine the law at two trials at *nisi prius* in Strafford County before Chief Justice Joel Parker of indictments for selling unlicensed liquor. Parker, who resigned from the bench in 1848 after fifteen years

---

[10] Curtis Memoir, Vol. I, 125–126, 135–136.

[11] Theodore Parker, *The Trial of Theodore Parker* (Boston 1855) (hereafter "Parker Trial"), 166: "... I rose and said, 'Do you want an answer to your question, sir?' ***When I offered to answer his question, he refused me the opportunity to reply!" Parker, who reproduces Curtis's speech in full, quotes Curtis as asking a single rhetorical question: "I should like to ask the reverend gentleman in what capacity he expects to be punished for his *perjury*?" (*Id.*; emphasis in original).

John Parker Hale
Courtesy of the Library of Congress,
Prints and Photographs Division, LC-USZ62-42393

on the Superior Court, New Hampshire's highest court, ten of them as Chief Justice, and served for the next twenty years as a professor at Harvard Law School, rejected Hale's argument in an extended ruling.

While the case was on appeal to the Superior Court, a newspaper and pamphlet war erupted on the issue. Hale published a pamphlet in his own name, in which he accused Chief Justice Parker of publishing an anonymous pamphlet report of the trials to justify his instructions to the jury; he set out the competing positions as follows:

> The rule of law as laid down by Chief Justice Parker is that "in civil cases the court judge of the law, and direct the jury

respecting it. The court are responsible for the correctness of the instructions, and the jury bound by them: and that the same rule in this respect, exists in criminal cases, which it is admitted exists in civil cases."

It is believed that in the progress of more than two centuries since the settlement of this State, this doctrine was first broached in Strafford County January 1842. And if the same practice obtains in *legal* as in geographical discoveries, of complimenting the discoverer by attaching his name to the newly discovered territory, this should be entitled pre-eminently "Judge Parker's law", for not only is he the first discoverer, but it is believed he is the first one who ever started on a voyage of discovery after such a principle in this latitude.[12]

Ultimately the convictions were affirmed by the New Hampshire Superior Court, Chief Justice Parker writing a lengthy concurring opinion.[13]

---

[12] John P. Hale, *Trial By Jury: Remarks on the Attempt by Chief Justice Parker to usurp the prerogative of the Jury in Criminal Cases* (Exeter 1842), 13. A fragment of the anonymous pamphlet to which Hale refers is in the Harvard College Library — apparently without a title page — and accessible on Google Books: *Reports of the Cases, The State v. Samuel Small, and the State v. Andrew Pierce, Jr. and others* (Concord 1842). The accuracy of Hale's legal position in criminal cases has been confirmed by highly respected recent scholarship. John Philip Reid, *Controlling the Law: Legal Politics in Early National New Hampshire* (NIU 2004), 119, 197–198.

[13] *Pierce v. State*, 13 N.H. 536, 554 (1843), aff'd as *The License Cases*, 46 U.S. 504 (1847). In the Supreme Court *Pierce* was one of three cases raising the same issue — whether state laws restricting the sale of liquor violated the Commerce Clause; in opening his argument Hale expressly acknowledged that the authority of the jury to determine the law was not before the Court. The other two cases arose in Rhode Island and Massachusetts; the petitioner in the latter was represented in the Supreme Court by Daniel Webster. A.J. King (ed.), *The Papers of Daniel Webster, Legal Papers, Volume 3, The Federal Practice* (Univ. Press of New England 1989), Part II, 681–692. Although the three cases were decided together, six Justices filed nine opinions.

United States of America.

Massachusetts District ss.

To the Marshall of our District of
Massachusetts, or either of his Deputies,
Greeting.

These are, in the name of the President
of the United States of America, to
command you the said Marshall
or Deputies, and each of you, forthwith to apprehend one Shadrach
now commorant in Boston in the said
District, a colored person, who is
alleged to be a fugitive from service
or labor, and who has escaped from
service or labor in the State of Virginia,
(if he may be found in your precinct)
and have him forthwith before me
one of the Commissioners of the Circuit
Court of the United States for the
Massachusetts District, at the Court
House in Boston aforesaid, then and
there to answer to the Complaint of
John Caphart, Attorney of John De Bree,
of Norfolk in the State of Virginia,

Commissioner Curtis's warrant to arrest Shadrach Minkins (1)
(National Archives, Waltham, MA)

alleging under oath, that the said
Shadrack owes service or labor to
the said De Bree in the said State
of Virginia, and while held to
service there under the Laws of the
said State of Virginia, escaped
into the State of Massachusetts aforesaid, and praying for the restoration
of the said Shadrack to the said
De Bree; and there and there before
me to be dealt with according to
law.

Hereof fail not, and make
due return of this Writ, with your
doings thereon before me.

Witness my hand and seal, at
Boston in the said District, on
this fourteenth day of February, in
the year of our Lord one thousand
eight hundred and fifty one.

Geo. T. Curtis
Commissioner of the
Circuit Court of the
United States for
Massachusetts District.

Commissioner Curtis's warrant to arrest Shadrach Minkins (2)
(National Archives, Waltham, MA)

Deputy Marshal's return on the warrant
(National Archives, Waltham, MA)

Endorsement on the warrant of adjournment of hearing
and escape of Shadrach Minkins
(National Archives, Waltham, MA)

CHAPTER III

"We Will Not Allow a Fugitive Slave
to be Taken from Massachusetts"

THE SHADRACH RESCUE

On February 14, 1851, George Ticknor Curtis, as "Commissioner of the Circuit Court of the United States for Massachusetts District," issued a warrant to the United States marshal for the district of Massachusetts:

These are in the name of the President of the United States of America, to command you the said Marshall, or Deputies, and each of you forthwith to apprehend one Shadrack, now commorant in Boston in the said District, a colored person, who is alleged to be a fugitive from service or labor — and who has escaped from service or labor — in the State of Virginia, (if he may be found in your precinct) and have him forthwith before me, one of the Commissioners of the Circuit Court of the United States for the Massachusetts District, at the Court House in Boston aforesaid, then and there to answer to the Complaint of John Caphart, Attorney for John De Bree of Norfolk in the State of Virginia, alleging under oath that the said Shadrack owes service or labor to the said De Bree in the said State of Virginia, and while held to service there under the Laws of the said State of Virginia escaped into the State of Massachusetts aforesaid, and praying for the restoration of the said Shadrack to the said De Bree...[1]

---

[1] Misc. Records of the United States Circuit Court for the District of Massachusetts, October 1852, National Archives, Waltham, MA. The language of the warrant is crucial to the subsequent discussion of the *Burns* Rescue cases, *infra*.

Lemuel Shaw
Courtesy of the Library of Congress,
Prints and Photographs Division, LC-USZ62-52119

A squad of deputy marshals arrested Shadrach at the Cornhill Coffee House the next day after he had served some of them breakfast and took him to the courthouse for an appearance before Commissioner Curtis.

Dana, Morris, Ellis Gray Loring, John G. King and other lawyers on the Vigilance Committee assembled in the commissioner's courtroom and applied for a three-day adjournment of the hearing. The papers on which the warrant issued were reviewed. Dana prepared a petition for a writ of *habeas corpus* — signed by Morris on behalf of Shadrach—to present to Chief Justice Lemuel Shaw, who rejected it summarily on the grounds that the prisoner himself had not signed it.[2]

When Dana returned to the commissioner's courtroom, the deputy marshals were in the process of clearing it of spectators and counsel, the adjournment having been granted by Commissioner Curtis, who endorsed the arrest warrant as follows:

> And now the hearing of the case being adjourned to Tuesday the eighteenth day of February instant, at ten o'clock in the forenoon, the said Deputy Marshall who has made return of this warrant, is hereby ordered to retain the said Shadrack in his custody, and have him before me the time last mentioned, at the Court House in Boston, for the further hearing of the complaint on which this warrant was issued.

Charles G. Davis, another of the Vigilance Committee counsel, and Elizur Wright, editor of the abolitionist daily *The Commonwealth*, were the last out of the courtroom, leaving Shadrach and the deputy marshals guarding him. At that moment, a group of black men forced the courtroom door wide open, pushed past the deputy marshals, and, as one of the deputies shouted "shoot him, shoot him," surrounded a stunned Shadrach and carried him out of the courthouse. Dana, back in his office, described what happened next:

> I returned to my office, & was planning out with a friend, the probable next proceedings, when we heard a shout from the Court House, continued into a yell of triumph, & in an instant after, down the steps came two huge negroes, bearing the prisoner between them, with his clothes half torn off, & so stupefied by the sudden rescue and the violence of his dragging off that he sat almost down, & I thought had fainted; but the men seised (sic) him, & being powerful fellows, hurried him through the Square into Court St., where he found the use of feet, & they went off

---

[2] *Ibid*; Robert F. Lucid (ed.), *The Journal of Richard Henry Dana, Jr.*, (Harvard 1968) Vol. II, 410–412 (hereafter "Dana Journal").

toward Cambridge, like a black squall, the crowd driving along with them & cheering as they went.[3]

Official outrage, particularly in Washington, was immediate. On February 18 President Millard Fillmore issued a proclamation calling upon the assistance of all "well-disposed Citizens" and

> commanding all officers, civil and military, and all other persons, civil or military, who shall be found within the vicinity of this outrage, to be aiding and assisting, by all means in their power, in quelling this, and other such combinations, and assisting the Marshal and his Deputies in recapturing the abovementioned prisoner; and I do, especially, direct, that prosecutions be commenced against all persons who have made themselves aiders or abettors in or to this flagitious offense; and I do further command, that the District Attorney for the United States, and all other persons concerned with the administration or execution of the Laws of the United States, cause the foregoing offenders, and all such as aided, abetted or assisted them, or shall be found to have harbored or concealed such fugitive, contrary to law, to be immediately arrested and proceeded with according to law.[4]

In Boston, the United States district attorney, George Lunt, and the marshal began rounding up persons thought to have been involved. The first arrested, on February 17, were the last two to leave the courtroom before the rescue — Charles G. Davis and Elizur Wright. [5] Two days later James Scott, a free black who sold used clothing, was arrested, followed on February 21 by the arrests of Alexander Burton, a free black

---

[3] Dana Journal 412.

[4] Webster Papers at 206–207.

[5] Collison, "This Flagitious Offense," *supra,* page xvii, n. 10, at 610–611. See generally Lawrence B. Goodheart, *Abolitionist, Actuary, Atheist: Elizur Wright and the Reform Impulse* (Kent State 1990); Elizur Wright, *The Sin of Slavery and Its Remedy* (New York 1833). The Shadrach rescue was not Wright's first brush with the law. *Commonwealth v. Elizur Wright,* 1 Cushing 46 (1848).

barber in Salem, and John K. Hayes, a white laborer. The next day Lewis Hayden[6] and Thomas Paul Smith, black clothing dealers, were arrested, and, finally on March 1, another black clothing dealer, John P. Coburn, and Robert Morris.[7]

Even as the arrests were going on, preliminary hearings were held on the charges against Wright and Davis.[8] The first, Elizur

---

[6] Hayden had been a slave in Kentucky whose father was sold away from the family and whose mother was so brutalized by a new owner for refusing "proposals of a base nature to her" that she lost her mind. Hayden's original master, a minister, sold him and his siblings at auction, having preached that "there was no more harm in separating a family of slaves than a litter of pigs." Later, Henry Clay, who had purchased Hayden's first wife and child at an estate sale, sold them to a slave trader. In 1842, aided by a white student at Oberlin, later a minister, Calvin Fairbank, and Fairbank's fiancée, Hayden and his new family escaped from Kentucky and finally made their way to Boston in 1846. Paul Runyon, *Delia Webster and the Underground Railroad* (Ky. 1996), 111–115; Stanley and Anita Robboy, "Lewis Hayden: From Fugitive Slave to Statesman," *New England Quarterly* (1973), Vol. 46, 591. Fairbank, who served two separate lengthy prison terms in Kentucky for slave rescues, is forgotten, despite his personal sacrifice.

[7] The juxtaposition of the arrests of Alexander Burton and Robert Morris requires comment, despite—or perhaps because of—the first article by Gary Collison on matters arising from the Shadrach rescue. "Alexander Burton and Salem's 'Fugitive Slave Riot' of 1851," *Essex Institute Historical Collections* (1992), Vol. 128, No. 1, 17, 18–19. The marshal's deputies arrested the wrong man—the person they wanted was "Andrew J. Burton," not Alexander, a man who was indicted but never found. On the afternoon of his arrest Lunt conceded that Alexander Burton was the wrong man, and he was released. And, as Collison reports, "before the end of February" Burton had filed a false arrest lawsuit in the Essex County Court against Lunt, seeking $10,000 in damages, and on February 26 Lunt was arrested, presumably on civil process, and released on $10,000 bail. What Collison seems not to have noticed is that the report of Burton's lawsuit in the March 1, 1851 issue of the *Salem Observer* identified counsel for Burton as John G. King and Robert Morris. It seems ill-considered on Morris's part to associate himself with the arrest of the United States district attorney at this sensitive juncture, and arguably the consequences to Morris were immediate: Lunt had Morris arrested three days later.

[8] The others who were taken up also had preliminary hearings. The *Twentieth Annual Report Presented to the Massachusetts Anti-Slavery*

Wright's, began on February 18 and was reported in the press.[9] Davis's, which began on February 20, was stenographically recorded and subsequently published.[10] At the conclusion of the hearing Commissioner Benjamin F. Hallett discharged Davis, who was represented by Richard Henry Dana, Jr., for want of probable cause. In Dana's *Morris* files there is a set of undated notes of what appears to be Morris's hearing before the Commissioner. The government's evidence was weak: witnesses placed Morris outside the courtroom before the crowd broke in and among the crowd and in a carriage in the street with several unidentified blacks after the rescue; no testimony implicated him as a active participant in the rescue. The two witnesses who gave the most incriminating testimony at Morris's trial did not appear at the preliminary hearing. However, Morris called no witnesses, and on the one-sided record the Commissioner chose to find the evidence of his involvement in Shadrach's escape sufficient.[11]

Indictments against all those named above except Davis and the wrong Burton were returned in the district court at its March term. The indictments are uniformly in the same fifteen counts, printed with blank spaces in which the defendant's name and occupation were entered in pen. Although the indictments do not specify the statutes under

---

Society by Its Board of Managers, January 28, 1852, with an Appendix (Boston 1852), 11, states that, after hearings, Commissioner Hallett bound all the individuals arrested for trial except Davis and Hayes.

[9] Elizur Wright files, Richard Henry Dana, Jr., Legal Papers, American Antiquarian Society, Worcester, Mass. (hereafter "Dana Papers"). Notes of the hearing also appear in the file.

[10] *Report of the Proceedings at the Examination [of] Charles G. Davis, Esq., on a Charge of Aiding and Abetting in the Rescue of a Fugitive Slave* (Boston 1851). The reference to Wright's examination is at page 8. There is also a discussion of the proceedings against Davis in the Dana Journal at 413–415.

[11] *Boston Daily Evening Transcript*, March 8, 1851; *Boston Courier*, March 10, 1851.

which the charges were laid,[12] the first twelve counts of the indictments arose under the Fugitive Slave Act 1850[13] and the last three under the Crimes Act of 1790.[14]

No arraignments of Smith or Hayes have been found. Coburn was apparently never arraigned on his indictment either, and the real Burton was never apprehended. Scott, Hayden, Morris and Wright were arraigned on their indictments on April 1, 1851.[15]

---

[12] Lunt explained the structure of the counts to Daniel Webster in his letter of March 31, 1851. Webster Papers at 221, 224. The reference to the Statute of "1799" is undoubtedly a transcription error.

[13] "Sec. 7, *And be it further enacted,* That any person who shall knowingly and willfully obstruct, hinder, or prevent such claimant, his agent, or attorney, or any person or persons lawfully assisting him, her or them, from arresting such fugitive from service or labor, either with or without process as aforesaid; or shall rescue, or attempt to rescue such fugitive from service or labor, from the custody of such claimant, his or her agent or attorney, or other person or persons lawfully assisting as aforesaid, when so arrested, pursuant to the authority herein given and declared; or shall aid, abet, or assist such person so owing service or labor as aforesaid, directly or indirectly, to escape from such claimant, his agent or attorney, or other person or persons, legally authorized as aforesaid...shall, for either of said offenses, be subject to a fine not exceeding one thousand dollars, and imprisonment not exceeding six months, by indictment or conviction before the district court of the United States for the district in which such offense may have been committed..."

[14] "Sec. 22. *And be it enacted,* That if any person or persons shall knowingly and willfully obstruct, resist or oppose any officer of the United States, in serving or attempting to serve any mesne process, or warrant, or any rule or order of any of the courts of the United States, or any other legal or judicial writ or process whatsoever, or shall assault, beat or wound any officer, or other person duly authorised in serving or executing any writ, rule, order, process or warrant aforesaid, every person so knowingly and willfully offending in the premises, shall, on conviction thereof, be imprisoned not exceeding twelve months, and fined not exceeding three hundred dollars."

[15] Although the indictments on file are not dated, on March 31 George Lunt wrote to Daniel Webster that "[t]he Grand Jury having, in fact, reported, and the Bills having been, in fact signed, only on Saturday last [March 29], between 2 and 3 p.m." Webster Papers 221, 223.

On April 19, all of the original indictments were nol prossed by the United States district attorney. Superseding indictments appear in the Archives for Robert Morris and Elizur Wright, on which they were arraigned on April 19 again; the change from the first indictment to the second was the addition of a new, lengthy count under the Fugitive Slave Act, bringing those up to counts one through thirteen, the Crimes Act counts being renumbered as counts fourteen through sixteen. No superseding indictments were located in the Archives for James Scott or Lewis Hayden, even though both were tried in June 1851.

THE SIMS RENDITION

On Thursday, April 3, 1851, another fugitive slave, Thomas Sims, was arrested in Boston and brought before Commissioner George Ticknor Curtis the next morning for a hearing on his rendition that lasted for two days. The following Monday, Richard Henry Dana, Jr., and Robert Rantoul, a Massachusetts Congressman, argued for a writ of *habeas corpus* in the Massachusetts Supreme Judicial Court; the application was rejected the same day in an opinion by Chief Justice Shaw upholding the constitutionality of the Fugitive Slave Act. A rescue from the courthouse was plotted but failed when bars were placed on the window of the room where Sims was confined.

Counsel for Sims made other applications for process to keep Sims in Boston on various pretexts and also filed an action in the United States circuit court against United States marshal Devens for damages and an injunction for false arrest. On the evening of April 10 counsel for Sims had applied *ex parte* to the United States circuit court for a writ of *habeas corpus* based on a criminal warrant against Sims for assault in resisting arrest separately issued by Commissioner Hallett. The writ was granted by Justice Levi Woodbury of the Supreme Court of the United States, who was then in Boston, returnable the following afternoon.

On the morning of April 11 Commissioner George Ticknor Curtis ordered Sims's removal.[16] Following a hearing on the afternoon of April 11 at which Benjamin Robbins Curtis represented Marshal Devens against claims of misconduct by Sims's counsel, Charles Sumner, Justice Woodbury denied relief and dismissed the proceeding.[17] On the 12th Sims was marched by troops to a ship to return him to Savannah.

Webster and President Fillmore could have dropped the Shadrach Rescue prosecutions at this point in time — and would have been wise to — without concern that doing so would prove that the Fugitive Slave Act was unenforceable in Boston. But Webster told the President on April 13: "Now, we need one thing further, viz, the conviction and punishment of some of the [Shadrach] rescuers."[18]

THE SHADRACH RESCUE TRIALS BEGIN

James Scott's trial began before Judge Peleg Sprague in the district court on May 28, 1851, and ended in a hung jury on June 6; Scott was identified as one of the group that forced open the courtroom door. Lewis Hayden's trial began that same day and also ended in a hung jury on June 17. Witnesses testified that Hayden had offered words of encouragement to Shadrach in the courtroom shortly before the rescue— "Don't be afraid—we will be with you till death", had helped Shadrach down the courthouse stairs, and had urged the crowd in the street to stand back so that Shadrach could get away.

---

[16] *Trial of Thomas Sims on an Issue of Personal Liberty* (Boston 1851); Thomas Higginson, *Cheerful Yesterdays* (Boston 1900), 143–144. "The Case of Thomas Sims," 14 *Monthly L. Rep.* 1 (1851); Leonard W. Levy, "Sims' Case: The Fugitive Slave Law in Boston in 1851," *Journal of Negro History* (1950), Vol. 35, 39.
[17] "The Case of Thomas Sims," *supra* n. 16, 11–14.
[18] Webster Papers 232–233.

Robert Morris's first trial began on June 17. On its second day, after some testimony had been taken,[19] the United States district attorney moved to disqualify one of the jurors who had been seated on the ground that he was biased against enforcement of the Fugitive Slave Act. Over defense objections Judge Sprague heard testimony of statements the juror had made on this score and then removed him from the jury, declaring a mistrial. On June 19, Judge Sprague, again over defense objections, adjourned the trial to the next term of the district court, Morris's recognizance bond being renewed with Josiah Quincy, Jr., sometime Mayor of Boston, as his co-obligor. On July 7, 1851, the district court made the following order in the *Morris* case:

> And it being the opinion of this Court that difficult and important questions of law are involved in this case, It is Ordered by the Court that this Indictment be remitted to the Circuit Court of this District, and that this order be entered on the minutes of this Court.[20]

At all three trials in the district court in May and June John P. Hale and Richard Henry Dana, Jr. represented the

---

[19] The June 20 issue of William Lloyd Garrison's newspaper, *The Liberator*, provided this vignette of Morris's abortive first trial:

> In the course of examination, Mr. Jackson, a member of the Suffolk bar, testified that the person who made the exclamation in the Court room, "Don't be afraid, we will stand by you!" on the day of the Shadrach rescue was several shades lighter than Hayden, upon which "pert Mr. Lunt" [the United States district attorney] inquired "if he did not know that the complexion of colored men changes one or two shades lighter when they are mad;" to which the witness made a negative reply. Mr. Dana, junior counsel for the prisoner, being desirous that the world should not lose the benefit of such a remarkable physiological fact, proposed to Mr. Lunt that he should confirm it by his testimony under oath, which Lunt declined to do, amid the laughter of the spectators."

[20] Morris file, U.S. circuit court, Oct. 1851. National Archives, Waltham, Mass. All further proceedings in these Rescue cases were held in the circuit court.

defendant. Dana needs no introduction here;[21] John P. Hale is one of that ever-growing group of lawyers now "almost unknown and forgotten by the profession which he once so greatly adorned". The newspaper accounts of the Shadrach Rescue cases reflect his considerable prowess as a trial lawyer in a high profile case and his resourcefulness in resisting an adversary on the bench at the second *Morris* trial who was far more skilled than his nominal opponent, George Lunt.

As Secretary of State, Webster had the responsibility for supervising the United States district attorneys nationwide, and Lunt was one he had no use for. In his letter of November 15, 1850, to the President, previously noted, he said that Lunt "has no talent, no fitness for his place, & no very good disposition." Webster had arranged for Rufus Choate, the dean of the Boston Bar, to prosecute the Rescue cases with Lunt, but on March 29, 1851, Choate withdrew, claiming conflicting engagements.[22] Webster told the President:

> I expect trouble, in finding proper counsel to assist Mr Lunt. The same reasons which induced Mr Choate to retire will probably induce others to be [un]willing to undertake. The truth is, Mr Lunt is not a very agreeable man to be associated with. He is not a good lawyer, theoretical or practical; and at the same time he is opinionated, self-willed and obstinate.[23]

At this juncture Webster wanted Benjamin Robbins Curtis to be lead counsel for the Government at the Rescue trials. But on April 9, 1851, Webster wrote to the President:

> I think we could manage to have the aid of B. R. Curtis' services, if his engagements allowed. But they do not. He is

---

[21] In addition to the three-volume set of his journal, edited and introduced by Robert F. Lucid, there are two full length biographies of Dana: Charles Francis Adams, *Richard Henry Dana, A Biography* (2 vols., Boston 1890) and Samuel Shapiro, *Richard Henry Dana, Jr. 1815–1882* (Michigan State 1961).

[22] Webster Papers 224–225.

[23] *Id.* at 229.

a member of the Legislature which is likely to sit till the middle of May; & after the Senate question is over, (if it ever shall be over) he is prepared for a public discussion, upon Administration matters. ***

The trials come on, the 28th instant. It is of great importance to convict Wright.[24]

In the end, Lunt tried the *Morris* case in the circuit court and the three trials preceding it with Nathaniel J. Lord of Salem.[25]

---

[24] *Id.* at 224 n. 3, 227, 230. The "Senate question" was the selection by the Legislature of a United States Senator from Massachusetts, in which, despite denouncing it as illegal and immoral, Curtis was unable to block Charles Sumner's election three weeks later. David Herbert Donald, *supra*, page 10, n. 20, 171 & n. 54.

[25] Lord, a prominent Salem lawyer, did not participate in either of Wright's trials in 1852. Dana recorded in his journal his conversation with Lord after the trials were over: "Speaking of the Rescue Cases, he let out his contempt for Lunt, without concealment. He said that after the two first disagreements, being at Washington, Webster said to him — 'I never heard much of the professional reputation of this Mr. Lunt. Can he get a conviction in these cases?'

Lord replied 'I think there is ev[idence] enough ag[ainst] two of them to warrant conviction.'

Webster. 'You don't answer my question, Sir.'

Lord. 'I did not mean to, Sir.'" (Dana Journal 533).

Benjamin Robbins Curtis
Courtesy of Collection of the Supreme Court of the United States

CHAPTER IV

"The Aid of B.R. Curtis' Services"

Circumstances came to involve Curtis in the Shadrach Rescue cases in quite an unexpected way. On September 4, 1851 Associate Justice Levi Woodbury of the Supreme Court of the United States died. Webster wrote to President Fillmore from Boston six days later:

> The general, perhaps I may say the almost universal sentiment here, is that the place should be filled by the appointment of Mr. B. R. Curtis. *** I recommend the immediate appointment of Mr. Curtis. *** You will see by the enclosed letter from Mr C. P. Curtis that Mr B. R. Curtis will accept the place, if offered to him.[1]

On September 22, President Fillmore gave Curtis a recess appointment as an Associate Justice of the Supreme Court. On October 7, Curtis thanked the President for the appointment, reminding him that there would be a term of the circuit court in Boston a week later and requesting an allotment to that Circuit so he could sit then.[2] He took the oath of office on October 10.

Curtis hit the ground running. On October 15, 1851, the first day of the term, Curtis delivered a charge to the grand jury substantially devoted to the crime of treason, defined so expansively that it is difficult to believe that he did not intend a shot across the bow of the Vigilance Committee, subject only to his carefully ambiguous qualification: "But what

---

[1] Webster Papers 272.
[2] Curtis Memoir 156.

amounts to the use of force, depends much upon the nature of the enterprise, and the circumstances of the case."[3]

Two weeks later, the retrial of Robert Morris began in the circuit court before Justice Curtis and Judge Sprague, sitting together. It was a reunion of sorts, and a situation of some ethical ambiguity. The reunion was of the participants in an earlier case, *Commonwealth v. Aves*,[4] in which Ellis Gray Loring, retained by the Anti-Slavery Society, successfully persuaded Chief Justice Shaw that a 6-year-old Louisiana slave girl, Med, automatically gained her freedom by being brought to Massachusetts; Benjamin Robbins Curtis represented the slave owner. At Morris's trial, Curtis was the presiding judge, and Loring and Chief Justice Shaw were defense witnesses, although Shaw's testimony was of little help to Morris.

The identity of a potential witness for the prosecution, George Ticknor Curtis, the Commissioner and brother of the presiding judge who had testified at all the earlier trials, including Morris's, raised a sensitive issue. Not only did he testify at both of the subsequent trials of Elizur Wright, there was no objection to his testimony at Morris's second trial. Although it was open to Judge Sprague to hold the circuit court alone, during Morris's trial Justice Curtis announced that his obligation to hold the circuit

---

[3] Charge to Grand Jury: Neutrality Laws and Treason, 30 F. Cas. 1024, 1025–26 (No. 18,269). A recent article, Dean Grodzins, "'Slave Law' versus 'Lynch Law' in Boston: Benjamin Robbins Curtis, Theodore Parker, and the Fugitive Slave Crisis, 1850–1855," *Massachusetts Historical Review* (2010) Vol. 1, 12–13, claims that "Curtis asked the grand jury to consider indicting the 'Shadrach rescuers' for treason." However, there is no evidence that these cases—in which indictments had been returned and superseded six months earlier and in which, in the two full trials already held, the Government had been unable to obtain convictions even for a misdemeanor—were re-presented to this subsequent grand jury. Furthermore, there is no suggestion that any rescuer was armed, that anyone was injured or even manhandled, or that any force was used except to push open the courtroom door. Surrounded by the crowd, Shadrach was moved out of the courtroom in their midst.

[4] 18 Pickering (35 Mass.) 193 (1836). See Leonard W. Levy, *The Law of the Commonwealth and Chief Justice Shaw* (Oxford 1957), 62–68.

Ellis Gray Loring
Charcoal and white chalk on paper by
Eastman Johnson, circa 1848.
Courtesy of Massachusetts Historical Society

court in Rhode Island would suspend further trials of the Rescue prosecutions at the current term of court.[5]

Finally, the Constitution limits the term of any recess appointment to the end of the next session of the Senate. Obviously, Justice Curtis contemplated that he would be nominated for a permanent position, and in fact President Fillmore did so on December 11, 1851. Justice John Paul Stevens has recently cautioned against the recess appointment of judges because of its inconsistency with the Constitutional

---

[5] *The Commonwealth*, November 6, 1851.

provision of tenure during good behavior, the guaranty of judicial independence. [6] Not only did Curtis face that risk in the abstract, Morris's counsel was one of the Senators who would be voting, after the trial was over, on whether Curtis should be confirmed for a permanent appointment on the Supreme Court. [7]

The first order of business on October 31, when Morris's second trial began, was his special plea, which challenged Judge Sprague's "remission" of the prosecution to the circuit court. The claim was in part statutory — an argument that Sections 1037 and 1038 of the Revised Statutes did not authorize such a remission after proceedings had already been had in the district court, as was the case here — and in part Constitutional — that Morris had been improvidently deprived of the timely conclusion of his prosecution by a verdict of the jury originally impanelled at his trial in the district court. Given the testimony Judge Sprague heard at the first trial of the bias against the Fugitive Slave Act attributed to the juror he removed, [8] his decision to do so would

---

[6] John Paul Stevens, *Five Chiefs: A Supreme Court Memoir* (New York 2011), 84–86.

[7] The Senate confirmed Curtis's appointment to the Supreme Court by a voice vote on December 20, 1851. Regrettably, the Senate Executive Journal does not break down the vote, much less identify the votes of individual Senators.

[8] Dana's *Morris* file contains a substantial clipping from the front page of the July 11, 1851 edition of *The Commonwealth*, reprinting "A Card" by Dana D. Walker, the juror Judge Sprague removed, purporting to quote from Dana's notes of the testimony at the hearing before Judge Sprague. One witness attributed to Walker such statements as: "[H]eard him say he thought the law entirely unconstitutional; and that no man ought to support it; *** the law ought to be resisted; that any man would be justified in resisting it, and that he would like nothing better than to be engaged in resisting it; would be willing to risk his life in it." Another witness said Walker said that "no slave ever could be carried out of Massachusetts" and that he was a member of the Vigilance Committee. A third witness testified that Walker "denounced the law as infernal, hellish, and unconstitutional; I have heard him say that the authors of the law ought to go to hell." Austin Bearse's *Reminiscences of Fugitive-Slave Law Days in Boston*

certainly pass muster today. [9] The defense position with respect to the correct construction of the statute was certainly arguable, but not indisputable. Justice Curtis devoted the first of his reported opinions in the *Morris* case to his reasons for denying the motion.

SHADRACH'S SLAVE STATUS

Judge Sprague was also certainly correct in finding satisfied the statutory requirement for remission to the circuit court that there be "difficult and important questions of law … involved in the case." What he must have had in mind was the nature and quantum of proof required to establish the statutory element of Section 6 of the Fugitive Slave Act that Shadrach "does in fact owe service or labor to the person or persons claiming him or her," or, as the superseding indictment charged, that Shadrach was "a person held to service and labor in a certain State of the United States, to wit, in the State of Virginia under the laws thereof and owing service and labor therein…"

The evidence at the Rescue trials — and Morris's was no different — fell into three segments: (1) proof of Shadrach's slave status; (2) proof of the defendant's behavior in the courthouse before the rescue; and (3) proof of the defendant's behavior in the street after Shadrach was out of the courthouse. The evidence on the first point was supplied by John De Bree, [10] who claimed Shadrach as his slave, and John Caphart, the slave catcher, mentioned earlier. Their testimony was much the same in all of the trials, although Caphart did not appear at Wright's first trial in June 1852.

(Boston 1880), at 5, lists Walker as a member of the Vigilance Committee.

[9] *Arizona v. Washington*, 434 U.S. 497, 512 (1978).

[10] De Bree came from a Norfolk, Virginia, family of some substance and served as a purser in the United States Navy. During the Civil War he was Chief of Bureau of the Office of Provisions and Clothing of the Confederate States Navy. J. Thomas Scharf, *History of the Confederate States Navy* (New York 1887), 819.

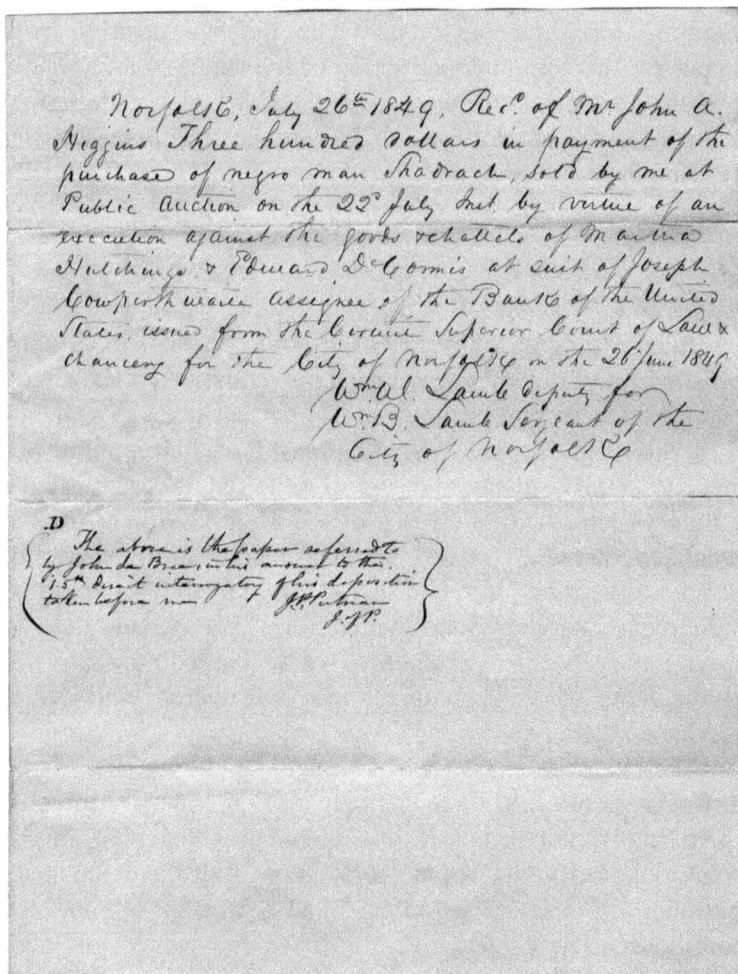

Norfolk Va. deputy's receipt for purchase money for Shadrach Minkins
(National Archives, Waltham, MA)

According to Justice Curtis's trial notes, over extended objection by the defense, De Bree testified that he had bought Shadrach in November 1849 from John Higgins and used him as a dining room servant; Shadrach absconded in May 1850. De Bree testified that he had never manumitted him and that "I hold him absolutely as my slave for life." He described Shadrach as "bacon color" and "darker than ordinary mulatto;"

Bill of sale of Shadrach Minkins to John De Bree
(National Archives, Waltham, MA)

the lightness of Shadrach's color — "not a regular black" — was the only point in the brief cross examination. [11]

De Bree was followed on the witness stand by Caphart, who testified that he had been a police officer in Norfolk for

---

[11] Benjamin Robbins Curtis, *Notes of cases before the Circuit Court*, Vol. 1, 190, 193–194, HLS MS 4042, Harvard Law School Library ("Curtis Trial Notes").

22 years. He had known Shadrach for sixteen years, first when he was the property of the Glenn estate. He also knew his father and had known the person called his mother for the last 10–12 years; she also belonged to the Glenn estate and was the wife of an old man named David. He had frequently heard Shadrach call them mother and father. Afterwards, he knew Shadrach as the property of Mrs. Hutchins. The Sheriff sold Shadrach to John A. Higgins; Caphart was present at the sale on the courthouse steps and put in his own bid for Shadrach. Later on he arrested him and put him in jail at Higgins's request. He also saw him at work in De Bree's house. He last saw him on February 15 in the Commissioner's courtroom, which he left when the case was adjourned.

On cross examination he testified that Shadrach was a "dark bacon color—between mulatto and black." He said that "as an officer, has had a great opportunity of knowing a great many blacks by arresting blacks. Done good deal of it—has been in the habit of arresting them & inflicting lashes on those who were sentenced, white & black—not often women. Has whipped by order of master." He also acknowledged that he had never seen Shadrach work at the Glenn estate, which he said was "fifty miles off."[12] This was the entirety of the

---

[12] Curtis Trial Notes 194–197. In *A Key to Uncle Tom's Cabin* (Boston 1853), at 5–8, Harriet Beecher Stowe treats Caphart as the paradigm for her fictional slave catcher, Haley, and reproduces a portion of a letter from Richard Henry Dana, Jr., describing his demeanor at the trials and assembling his testimony "[f]rom the Examination of John Caphart, in the 'Rescue Trials,' at Boston in June and Nov., 1851 and October, 1852."
Question. Is it part of your duty, as a policeman, to take up coloured persons who are out after hours in the streets?
Answer. Yes, Sir.
Q. What is done with them?
A. We put them in the lock-up, and in the morning they are brought into court and ordered to be punished, — those that are to be punished.
Q. What punishment do they get?
A. Not exceeding thirty-nine lashes.
Q. Who gives them the lashes?
A. Any of the officers. I do, sometimes.
Q. Are you paid *extra* for this? How much?

testimony about Shadrach's slave status, which was a major legal issue for the defense at the 1851 trials.

The issue came to a head on a defense objection during De Bree's testimony. Dana's research showed that an action under Section 6 of the Fugitive Slave Act required proof that "the person so arrested does in fact owe service or labor to the person or persons claiming him or her, in the State or Territory from which such fugitive may have escaped as aforesaid...." [13] Building upon this, Hale argued that under the applicable Virginia statutes, Shadrach was only legally a slave if his descent from a female who had been a slave in 1785 were established. In addition, Hale relied on cases from Dana's research which created evidentiary presumptions of

---

A. Fifty cents a head. It used to be sixty-two cents. Now it is fifty. Fifty cents for each one we arrest, and fifty more for each one we flog.

Q. Are these persons you flog, men and boys only, or are they women and girls also?

A. Men, women, boys, and girls, just as it happens. ***

Q. Is your flogging confined to those cases? Do you not flog slaves at the request of their masters?

A. Sometimes I do. Certainly, when I am called upon.

Q. In these cases of private flogging, are the negroes sent to you? Have you a place for flogging?

A. No, I go round, as I am sent for.

Q. Is this part of your duty as an officer?

A. No, sir.

Q. In these cases of private flogging, do you inquire into the circumstances, to see what the fault has been, of if there is any?

A. That's none of my business. I do as I am requested. The master is responsible.

Q. In these cases, too, I suppose you flog women and girls, as well as men?

A. Women and men.

Q.. Mr. Caphart, how long have you been engaged in this business?

A. Ever since 1836.

Q. How many negroes do you suppose you have flogged, in all, women and children included?

A. [*Looking calmly around the room.*] I don't know how many niggers you have got here in Massachusetts, but I should think I have flogged as many as you have got in the State.

[13] *Hill v. Low*, 12 F. Cas. 172 (E.D. Pa. 1822) (No. 6,494) (Washington, J.)

freedom or slave status depending upon the blackness of the person alleged to be a slave.[14] It was here that Shadrach's mulatto status was crucial. The testimony of De Bree and Caphart established only that Shadrach was held as a slave. However, more was required to rebut the presumption of freedom — or, depending on the jurisdiction, to carry the burden of slave status — arising from Shadrach's mulatto coloring, particularly in the absence of testimony concerning the wooliness of his hair and the flatness of his nose. The heading to the list of precedents in Dana's notes is "Possession is nothing."

Whether Judge Sprague made a formal ruling on this issue at the trials of Scott or Hayden does not survive, and of course Justice Curtis would not have been bound by such a ruling had it occurred. However, since this was a necessary issue for the jury, Judge Sprague's charge did address it. At Scott's trial, Judge Sprague had instructed the jury:

> Did Shadrach owe service? A prayer has been put in by the defense for instruction as to color. It was true that by the law of Virginia, a person of Shadrach's color would be free; evidence must therefore exist upon this point.

> It had been objected that in a case of liberty and slavery possession was not conclusive evidence against a party sueing [sic] for freedom. However, that was in a case where one person sues for his liberty, it was not the case here. Shadrach is no party to this proceeding. Shadrach, after the decision of this case, has still the right to sue for his liberty.

> If Debree and Caphart's testimony is to be believed, there being no evidence on the other side to conflict with it, then Shadrach was a slave. That he was a fugitive from service

---

[14] *Hudgins v. Wrights*, 1 Hen. & Munford (11 Va.) 134 (1806)(per St. George Tucker, J.); *Gober v. Gober* [sometimes *Gobu v. Gobu*], 1 Taylor's Reports 164, 2 Haywood's Reports 170 (N.C. 1802); *Adelle v. Beauregard*, 1 Martin's Reports 99 (La. 1810); *State v. Davis*, 2 Bailey 558 (S.C 1831); *Gentry v. McMinnis*, 3 Dana 382 (Ky. 1835); *Gatliff's Adm'r v. Rose,* 8 B. Monroe 629 (Ky. 1848). Dana's case files contain more than one set of his handwritten notes on this subject.

and labor while in this State, must be judged of by the fact that there was no evidence that he was emancipated or transported. He therefore owed service at the time of the rescue.[15]

Although he was not bound to do so, at the *Morris* trial Justice Curtis adopted and elaborated on the position taken earlier by Judge Sprague, who was sitting next to him on the bench. Judge Sprague had undoubtedly warned him of what was coming, as Justice Curtis's trial notes, next to his list of the authorities cited in oral argument, add the statement in the margin: "Hale says that all suits for freedom except one." This observation was crucial to Justice Curtis, because, in his opinion announced at least preliminarily at the trial on November 6, it was the distinction he employed — incorrectly — to deprive Morris of the protection of the evidentiary inference these cases provided.[16] In his opinion as reported, Justice Curtis dismissed the authorities cited by Hale as arising in "suits which directly involve the freedom of one of the parties" and stated that:

> The courts, not only of Virginia, but of other slave states, seem to have treated suits for freedom as a distinct class of cases, not controlled by some of the rules which are ordinarily administered, but entitled to a kind of favor, not extended to any other legal proceeding. Vaughan v. Phebe, Mart. & Y. 5 [1827]; [*Hudgins v. Wrights*], 1 Hen. & M. 134.

---

[15] *The Commonwealth*, June 6, 1851. The quoted portion of Judge Sprague's jury instructions comes at the end of his lengthy presentation on the Constitutionality of the Fugitive Slave Act, which is reported as *United States v. Scott*, 27 F. Cas. 990 (No. 16,240b) (June 1851), and which omits the portion of the instructions addressing the specifics of Scott's guilt or innocence. It is derived from the scrapbooks of Judge Samuel Rossiter Betts of the Southern District of New York, meaning that in its original form it was from a newspaper publication. The *Commonwealth* report of Judge Sprague's charge at the *Hayden* trial is to the same effect but too abbreviated to be of any value to this analysis.
[16] *The Commonwealth*, November 7, 1851.

But I have looked in vain for cases tending to show that whenever the fact of slavery, under the law, is put in issue, in a proceeding other than a suit for freedom, any rules of evidence are administered anywhere, except such as are applicable to similar facts in cases at the common law.[17]

At this point Justice Curtis proceeded to rely on cases which hold the opposite of the proposition which he had just advanced. The first, which he correctly characterized as "a suit for freedom," was *Mima Queen and Child v. Hepburn*, 11 U.S. 290, 295–297 (1813), but in it Chief Justice Marshall sustained the lower court's refusal to admit hearsay pedigree evidence because to do so would establish "the application of a rule of evidence to cases of this description, which would be inapplicable to general cases in which a right to property may be asserted."[18]

Similarly, *Miller v. Denman*, 8 Yeager 233, 234–236 (Tenn. 1835), also relied on by Justice Curtis, was an action for damages by Denman, a slaveholder, against Miller "for enticing out of the possession and service of the plaintiff, a slave, named Harriet, the defendant knowing her to be the property of the plaintiff." The defendant Miller wished to introduce evidence of Harriet's straight hair and fair complexion to establish that, enticed or not, she was not legally a slave and therefore not the property of Denman. Referring specifically to the *Vaughn* case cited by Justice Curtis as support for Miller's offer of proof, in dictum the Tennessee Supreme Court said:

This principle is distinctly asserted by this court, in the case of Vaughan vs. Phebe, Mart. & Yerb. 5. Although that case extends the right to introduce hearsay evidence to the utmost limit, and fur[ther] than other courts of high

---

[17] *Morris* at 1329–1330 (footnote omitted).

[18] In dissent, Justice Duvall contended for the application of the very principle — relaxation of the rules of evidence in a case involving freedom — which Chief Justice Marshall and Justice Curtis rejected. See R. Kent Newmyer, *John Marshall and the Heroic Age of the Supreme Court* (LSU 2001), 426–429.

authority have gone; yet, as the case was fully argued, and maturely considered by the court, and has been acquiesced in ever since that decision was made, we will not now disturb it.[19]

Then, moving to the issue on appeal, the same one Justice Curtis treated as dispositive, the Court went on to say:

But the counsel for Denman insists, and so the court charged the jury, that although this evidence might be admissible in a suit by the girl against Denman for her freedom, yet the defendant is not entitled to its benefit in this action. And why is he not?"

The Court ruled that the defendant was so entitled and reversed the judgment of the court below, holding, *id.* at 237:

The question, therefore, recurs, whether evidence of the possession and claim of ownership of a human being by a plaintiff is sufficient proof to entitle him to a recovery in this action. We think it is not. There must be some proof that such human being is a slave. And while dark complexion and woolly head would constitute *prima facie* that proof; the fair complexion, straight hair, would repel the conclusion, and hence a resort to other proof would be necessary. In the investigation of fact necessarily involved in the controversy, the same evidence by which it would be lawful to establish it in a controversy for the freedom of the girl, would be proper in this action.

Plainly Justice Curtis did not follow the authorities on which he claimed to base his decision: with the single, acknowledged outlier of *Vaughan v. Phebe*, suits for freedom enjoyed no special evidentiary relaxation, and Morris should have been allowed whatever burden-shifting benefit he could

---

[19] *Id.* at 236. *Vaughan v. Phebe* sustained, in an action for her freedom by a woman held as a slave, the admission in evidence of a judgment for the same relief against a different owner obtained by her mother's sister, who established her right to freedom on account of her descent from Native American ancestry.

claim under the laws of Virginia from the evidence of Shadrach's physiognomy.[20] Moreover, even if Justice Curtis had been right in concluding that the rules of evidence were relaxed only in "a suit for freedom," it is hard to see why a different rule should apply in a case where the prosecution sought to take away the freedom of a criminal defendant and had the burden of proof beyond a reasonable doubt.

To be sure, Justice Curtis's analysis arose on an objection to the testimony of De Bree about his former possession and claim of ownership of Shadrach; *Miller* does not hold that such evidence must be excluded. Rather, *Miller* simply holds that it is inadequate to prove slave status, as does *Hudgins*. But Justice Curtis held not only that it was admissible, but that "if not controlled, sufficient to establish that Shadrach was held to service under the laws of Virginia when he escaped from that state." Thus he was prepared to allow the jury to conclude that Shadrach was legally a slave from proof that "this person was bought and sold and treated as a slave," exactly the kind of circular question begging rightly exposed by recent scholarly analysis.[21] He also rejected the necessity for proving Shadrach's pedigree back to a slave on the maternal side in 1785 on the basis that since evidence of precisely the same quality would be used in that inquiry, "why is it not also competent, in the first case, to prove a state of slavery of Shadrach in 1849?"

---

[20] Thomas D. Morris, *Southern Slavery and the Law, 1619–1860* (UNC 1996), 26.

[21] Ariela J. Gross, "Litigating Whiteness: Trials of Racial Determination in the Nineteenth-Century South," 108 *Yale L.J.* 109, 163 (1998); *id., What Blood Won't Tell: A History of Race on Trial in America* (Harvard 2008), 54. Even Dana, who sometimes had praise for Curtis, commented to his diary: "We labored this point, & were much disappointed by his decision. I cannot believe it to be right, & his reasons rather confirmed my opinion. They were small & second rate." Dana Journal 466.

THE EVIDENCE AT TRIAL
OF MORRIS'S CULPABILITY

The deputy marshals and constables assisting them, a reporter and the clerk described what went on in the courtroom during and before the rescue, including the statement by one black spectator to Shadrach that "we will stand by you to the death", after which Shadrach removed his coat, rolled up his sleeves, "& adjusted his cravat", saying: "If I die, I die like a man". However, they offered no testimony incriminating of Morris. They saw Morris — and other counsel — in the courtroom, speaking to the prisoner, prior to the rescue; Morris also went in and out of the courtroom several times. At the time of the rescue, Morris was not in the courtroom and was last seen in it at the time the order to clear it was given, following the adjournment. [22] Two witnesses claimed that, coming down the stairs from the courtroom, a smiling Morris shook his finger — or his head, depending on the witness — at a constable he knew who was coming up the stairs as the crowd was forcing the courtroom door.[23]

Outside the courthouse, a witness saw a man come out of the courthouse door and signal with a baton:

> [A]fter the beckon there was a rush from the court and Ct. Street to the door whence the man came who beckoned — 50 or 60 col'd people & quite a portion came into the door and instantly rushed back again. After quite [a] number came out a person appeared without hat & my belief without a coat & one man hold of him each side. They rushed into Court St....[24]

James Andrews, a fifteen-year-old who worked in the Clerk's Office, testified that before the rescue Morris came out of the courtroom two or three times to talk to black people outside in the hall. [25]

---

[22] Curtis Trial Notes 197–212.
[23] *Ibid.*, 213–216.
[24] *Ibid.*, 212–213.
[25] *Ibid.*, 216–218.

The next witness, Ellis Wright, described the flight of Shadrach and the crowd from the courthouse, turning onto Garden Street:

> They came to a halt opposite Dailey's stable & a cab was standing there & 3 [people] and the fugitive rushed into the cab — Some cried it would not do [-] take him out.

Wright heard glass break. Wright did not identify Morris, but he was followed on the stand by William Bailey, who witnessed three or four men in the cab on Garden Street and the breaking of the glass on one of the cab's doors. He testified: "Morris was in the cab. *** I am sure I saw him in the cab." However, he conceded on cross examination that he had not seen the occupants of the cab either get in or get out of it. Two other witnesses testified to seeing Morris in the cab and getting out of it; one claimed to have seen him get in, as well.[26] The last two witnesses provided the most incriminating testimony. Newell Harding, Jr., a seventeen-year-old, testified that after the glass broke in the coach, Shadrach and Morris walked side by side down the street, Morris's arm on Shadrach's back. John Mack, a fifteen-year-old, testified that when Morris came out of the courtroom a second time, "a col'd man ask'd him how many in Ct Room. M[orris] said 7 or 8 white men & I think he sd a good time or good chance, I could not be certain which he sd but I am certain he sd one or the other." In addition, following the crowd surrounding Shadrach out into the street, Mack testified that: "The crowd was a little ahead of Morris. Near Grant's house crowd hauled up & he took off his hat and shook it & sd go ahead men." Here the Government rested its direct case.[27]

The defense began with an opening by Dana. He pointed out that Morris had not only been involved in the effort to free Shadrach legally, by the *habeas corpus* application to Chief Justice Shaw, Morris was also aware of a defect in the

---

[26] *Ibid.*, 218–227.
[27] *Ibid.*, 229–234.

Richard Henry Dana, Jr.
Courtesy National Park Service,
Longfellow House-Washington's Headquarters National Historic Site

Virginia record which gave Shadrach "a good chance" to avoid rendition. On the facts, Dana said that the evidence showed that the rescue was spontaneous, not concerted, and that Morris had been a bystander: "Morris was going to his office & had arrived at the corner of Court Sq. and Ct. St. & hearing a shout he followed. He was not in the cab." Dana argued that under the Fugitive Slave Act it would be necessary to prove Shadrach was a slave by the laws of Virginia. He also asserted that the Fugitive Slave Act was, first, unconstitutional and, second, inapplicable by its terms to the order with which the rescue had interfered: Commissioner Curtis's remand order to the deputy U.S. marshal when the hearing was adjourned. With regard to the last three counts of the indictment, he argued that the Fugitive Slave Act of 1850 had repealed the Crimes Act of 1790 to the extent that the latter might have applied on the facts of this case. He concluded by referring to "the right of the jury to judge of the law" irrespective of oath the jurors had taken.[28]

The defense began calling its witnesses, starting with thirteen character witnesses including Josiah Quincy, Jr., who had been Mayor of Boston until two years before. These were followed by the testimony of Ellis Gray Loring, who began by testifying to his very intimate thirteen-year acquaintance with Morris, who was "[e]xcellent in every particular." Loring said that he had arranged for Morris to represent Shadrach at Shadrach's request and described Morris's various comings and goings from the courtroom at Loring's request, including in connection with the execution of the *habeas corpus* petition. Loring also said that on examination of the court papers, he had found "essential defects of form" which had been discussed in front of Morris, testimony subsequently confirmed and explained by Charles G. Davis.[29] Loring was

---

[28] *Ibid.*, 235–240.

[29] *Ibid.*, 241–245, 247–249. *The Commonwealth*, November 7 and 8, 1851. Section 6 of the Fugitive Slave Act prescribed the documentation to be laid before the Commissioner to obtain a warrant as a "deposition or affidavit, in writing, to be taken and certified by such court, judge or commissioner or by other satisfactory testimony, duly taken and certified by some court, magistrate, justice of the peace or other legal officer authorized to administer an oath and take depositions under the laws of the State or Territory from which such person owing service or labor may have escaped, with a certificate of such magistracy or other authority, as aforesaid, with the seal of the proper court or officer thereto attached..." According to Curtis's notes, Davis said: "These papers did not purport to be a transcript of any record but were original affts. & there was no statement it was a transcript[,]... that this was a court of record & no sufficient certificate that the person was a judge — also the authentication of the power of Atty." The documents are in the 1852 miscellaneous circuit court records at the National Archives branch in Waltham, Mass., and do include an original affidavit by De Bree. Whether Davis's objections would have carried the day is another matter.

followed by Chief Justice Shaw, who recalled denying the *habeas corpus* petition but had no recollection of Morris's having been present.[30]

Following this testimony, the defense called witnesses who raised doubts about the Government's evidence — one who had been on the stairs at the time Morris was supposed to have come down smiling and shaking his finger but did not see Morris; another who said Morris's conversation outside the court room concerned the adjournment and did not include anything about a rescue; a third who said that he had heard Morris discuss in the corridor where Shadrach was likely to be confined pending the hearing on the adjourned date; a fourth who heard Morris tell blacks in the hall not to pull on the courtroom door.[31]

Moving outside of the courthouse, the defense called a witness who saw Morris walking in a leisurely fashion in front of the courthouse in a different direction from the crowd; another witness who walked with Morris "3 ½ rods" (more than fifty feet) behind Shadrach and got a frosty reply to his enthusiastic comment on the rescue; four witnesses to the incident with the cab, including its driver, who testified either affirmatively that Morris was not there or that they did not recognize him as having been there; and a witness who placed Morris elsewhere as the crowd passed.[32] There was a reasonable doubt.

SUMMATIONS

Hale made the most of his opportunities. He started by characterizing slavery as "that sin which has brought such woes upon this country," which "comes into your Court House to-day, with a brazen face, and asks you to declare that a human being is a slave. And this you have got to do." He hinted at the argument the Court would stop him from making

---

[30] *Ibid.*, 246.
[31] *Ibid.*, 252–258.
[32] *Ibid.*, 258–271.

later — that the jury was the judge of the law — but here he framed it in terms of the jury having the entire responsibility in the case: "The responsibility of finding a true verdict is imposed on you by the Constitution; and every thing, I hold, that enters into the issue of Guilty or Not Guilty, *you* are to find, and nobody else."

He then moved on to the element of slavery:

[W]as Shadrach the slave whom Debree bought in Norfolk? How do they prove it? John Caphart says he was.

I don't believe it. Caphart's business is catching and whipping negroes, and I don't think he is very scrupulous how he gets them. He comes into Court, and seeing the poor wretch sitting here in Court with an officer on each side, and he says, "Yes, he is the man." Why did not they go to the Cornhill Coffee-house with John Caphart ? He is not entitled to a moment's credit here. He is a **woman-whipper**. That is what John Caphart is! He tells you so; that he whips, without regard to *sex* or *color*. He is a walking scourge, and has followed the trade for 22 years. *This* is a man who contaminates this Court House and this air of Massachusetts that he breathes. Government asks you to give up one of your citizens, because *such* a man says he is a slave, and to punish Robert Morris for aiding him, *as they say*, to escape. *** [T]his ... government will fine and imprison him who, they say, would give freedom to one man. [Some murmur of feeling being heard in the Court, the Marshal orders silence.] Yes! silence in the Court! Silence the beating of your hearts when you hear such things. If the case required it, I might stop here. You could say to the Government, if you want to get [a] conviction here, bring other witnesses than such as *John Caphart*! This is not only the worst kind of evidence, but the worst of the kind.[33]

Curtis's notes add: "Caphart's business is to deal in agony —."[34]

---

[33] *The Commonwealth*, November 8, 1851.
[34] Curtis Trial Notes 273.

Hale focused on the weakness of the prosecution's claim that there had been a conspiracy to rescue Shadrach. He attacked the credibility of the deputy marshals but called their testimony "of little consequence." He treated the testimony of the witnesses to what transpired inside the courthouse the same way, explaining Mack's testimony about Morris's assertion of "a good chance" as referring "a fatal mistake" found by counsel in the papers. For the conflicting evidence of what happened outside the courthouse after the rescue, Hale pointed out that Mack had admitted on cross that he had followed the crowd out of the courthouse to the cab but could not identify Morris in it, and that the other Government witnesses who had identified him had either no acquaintance with him or purported to have seen him through the broken glass of the cab. For the witness who saw Morris with his arm across Shadrach's shoulders, Hale argued that, if that were the case, more people would have seen it.

Hale moved on to argue that the jury was to judge the facts as well as the law, but Justice Curtis stopped him from arguing that issue to the jury, later rendering an opinion on this issue discussed below. Even so, Hale was permitted to argue it to the Court in front of the jury. His summation was ended in the peroration:

> You are to find that Shadrach was a **slave** on that day, when he stood in this room. You have got to *swear* he was a **slave**! that a man whom God made, and whom Christ redeemed was a **slave**, a *thing*, and not a **man**! and you have got to find that there was a conspiracy, because parties here intimated to officers of this Court that there was a God in Heaven who would judge them for their works.
>
> May the gracious assisting spirit and presence of the Lord God Omnipotent, the Governor of Heaven and Earth and all things therein contained, go along with you, give you counsel and decide you to do that which is just and for his glory.[35]

---

[35] *The Commonwealth*, November 10, 1851.

Lunt's summation, as reported, emphasized his conspiracy claim, "and it mattered not whether it was concocted a week before or within but a few moments of the time when it was carried into execution." He pointed to Shadrach's statement in the courtroom, and he argued that the absence of proof that Morris spoke with Shadrach after the deputy marshals had cleared others from the room proved that he was there for a different purpose — aiding the rescuers who were about to burst in. He emphasized Mack's testimony of Morris's conduct both inside and outside the courthouse and claimed that Mack's testimony had not been impeached. He also argued the three positive identifications of Morris in the cab and the testimony that Morris had walked with his arm around Shadrach; as to the latter he said: "If he has done nothing else, this, which is not contradicted, is aiding and assisting the escape of Shadrach."[36]

JURORS AS JUDGES OF THE LAW

The summations were completed on Saturday, November 8. The Court did not sit on Sundays or on November 10, which was Election Day. On the morning of November 11, Justice Curtis delivered his opinion rejecting Hale's argument on the jury's power to judge the law and proceeded to charge the jury that it was obligated to follow the Court's instructions on the law.[37]

Hale's argument exists in three versions: the report in *The Commonwealth,* the notes of the trial taken by Justice Curtis and Dana's notes. Justice Curtis's notes record Hale's opening argument as follows:

> It is the undoubted prerogative of the jury to pass on the law —

---

[36] *Id.*
[37] *The Commonwealth,* November 13, 1851.

> Not willing that it should pass that ever admitted that the
> jury should [not] take the whole issue – whatever may be
> the opinion of the court. It is also the right of the prisoner.
> Jury cannot put off their responsibility.

There follows a list of the authorities Hale relied on: the
opinion of the New York Supreme Court in *People v.
Croswell*, Alexander Hamilton's argument in *Croswell*, the
section from Littleton and Coke on Littleton cited in Justice
Kent's opinion in *Croswell*, the decision of the United States
Supreme Court in *Georgia v. Brailsford*, the Sedition Act of
1798, *Fries'* Case and the charges in the impeachment of
Justice Chase based on it, the Massachusetts Supreme Judicial
Court's decisions in *Commonwealth v. Knapp* and *Common-
wealth v. Kneeland*, the Maine Supreme Court's decision in
State v. Snow, and the Trial of John Lilburne in 1649.[38]

Justice Curtis records Hale's subsequent argument as
follows:

> No controversy in Eng'd since Mr. Fox's bill as to the right
> of Juries. Reads from 1 Erskine's speeches 117. Better
> abolish the jury if have no duty &&. Juries did the whole
> formerly and *Judges Norman Intruders.*

> It is a great & important question & ought to be treated
> with the utmost respect.

> The law is in a chrysalis state — asks the court to go back
> to the earliest formulations of the law.[39]

---

[38] *People v. Croswell*, 3 Johnson's Cases 337 (N.Y. 1804); *State of
Georgia v. Brailsford*, 3 U.S. 1 (1794); *Commonwealth v. Knapp*, 27
Mass. 477 (1830); *Commonwealth v. Kneeland*, 37 Mass. 206 (1838);
State v. Snow, 18 Maine Reports 346 (1841). These were the same
authorities he had relied on in *Pierce* almost ten years earlier in New
Hampshire. The reference in the paragraph below to "Erskine's
speeches", depending on the edition Hale was using, is probably to
his argument on the rights of juries in the *Dean of St. Asaph's Case*
in 1784.
[39] Curtis Trial Notes 277.

Dana's notes add nothing beyond a specific reference to Justice James Kent's opinion in *Croswell* and the citation of the trial of William Penn. *The Commonwealth*'s account, preceding the list of citations, is:

> *Mr. Hale* then turned to the Court. Desiring first the acquittal of Robert Morris, he desired it not so much as he did securing the sacred rights of the trial by Jury. He held it to be the right of the Jury to decide on the law and the facts. He entertained an undoubted conviction that on a review of the facts, the Jury would acquit the prisoner. But he would not have it pass, even by implication, that he admitted that the Jury should not take the *whole issue*, law and fact, into their hands. And this there was abundant authority to sustain. *Mr. Hale* protested that it was a usurpation on the part of the Court to preclude the addressing of this to the Jury, but disclaimed any imputation on the Court. Nothing was further from his intention than to be disrespectful to the Court. [*The Court* were ready to listen themselves to Mr. Hale's views on this subject, but could not permit it to be addressed to the Jury.] *Mr. Hale* continued that he held that everything involved in the issue of guilty or not guilty was for the Jury; they were to take the whole matter into their own hands; the responsibility was on them and their consciences, and they cannot put it off.

And after listing his authorities, according to the newspaper account:

> Mr. Hale entreated the Court to weigh well this question, before they made a decision that was to be law in this District. The doctrine claimed as its defenders in England, the names of Coke, of Littleton, and of Blackstone, and in this country the names of Hamilton, of Kent, of Shaw. He asked that the Court should not throw its influence into the scales of Power against Right! Do not set up a precedent that, in other times, bad men may follow. Let the enlightened humanity of this Court give its sanction to the odious principle maintained by the Government, and it will entrench itself, where it may, perhaps, never be shaken — but let it sanction the great fundamental principle of liberty that we maintain.

Given Curtis's speech in Faneuil Hall almost exactly one year earlier, Hale must have known that there was absolutely no chance he would succeed with this argument. Hale's deployment of it at the *Morris* trial is the more striking because it was the first time that it had been made in the Rescue trials, even though he could not have been any worse off making it to Judge Sprague in the two completed trials Judge Sprague presided at alone in May and June 1851.[40]

The length alone of his opinion on the subject — delivered just three days after Hale made his argument, Lunt's desultory response to the jury quickly cut off by the Court — suggests that Justice Curtis expected it; he cited *Pierce* and presumably he knew of Hale's pamphlet. But the elaborate and largely irrelevant analysis, dominating his opinion, of the supposed inconsistency of a jury's power to judge the law with the uniformity contemplated by the Constitutional structure of the federal government and particularly the Supremacy Clause was unresponsive both to Hale's argument and to his authorities. Moreover, except for the preamble to Justice Curtis's opinion in Volume I of Curtis's Reports, printed in 1854, there is nothing in any record of his summation suggesting that Hale was attacking the Constitutionality of the Fugitive Slave Act in his closing argument, a predicate of Justice Curtis's opinion; Hale's point was here quite different. By creating this strawman, Justice Curtis dodged the distinction which even Justice Samuel Chase recognized in his debate with William Wirt at the *Callender* trial and in his instructions to the jury: that there

---

[40] The issue apparently did come up, though. Dana's Hayden file contains his draft of a handwritten letter to Judge Sprague, dated July 11, 1851, apparently commenting on a draft report of "the points decided by yourself, in the rescue cases" which regrettably seems neither to have been printed nor survived in another form. In it Dana quotes a portion of Judge Sprague's jury instructions:

> The jury is to determine what are the facts, & the judge to determine what is the law. You must take the case as it is given by the Court. You are to say, in response to a single question, whether the Dft has or has not done the acts. Your only inquiry is *whether the facts exist*, as set forth in the indictment.

was a dispositive jurisprudential distinction between the jury's then-recognized right to judge the law on the facts proved — which Justice Chase admitted and is all Hale was asking for — and any right to have the jury determine the Constitutionality of a statute, which Wirt contended for and Justice Chase denied.[41]

When he moved on to address Hale's authorities, Justice Curtis went from bad to worse. Largely on the basis that "I cannot help feeling much doubt respecting the accuracy of this report," Justice Curtis simply disregarded as authority the Supreme Court's decision in *Georgia v. Brailsford*. Although *Brailsford* was only a civil action, Justice Curtis acknowledged that Chief Justice Jay reportedly instructed the jurors that "they have the *right* to take upon themselves to determine the law as well as the fact" and, Justice Curtis might have added,

---

[41] In the argument appears the following dialogue:

> Judge Chase. — No man will deny your law — we all know that juries have the right to decide the law, as well as the fact — and the Constitution is the supreme law of the land, which controls all laws which are repugnant to it.

> Mr. Wirt. — Since then, the jury have a right to consider the law, and since the constitution is law, the conclusion is certainly syllogistic, that the jury have a right to consider the Constitution.

> Justice Chase. — A *non sequitur*, Sir.

> Here Mr. Wirt sat down.

Justice Chase later charged the jury as follows, citing to the language of the Sedition Act, which Hale did rely on:

> ... I understand that a right is given to the jury to determine what the law is in the case before them; and not to decide whether a statute of the United States produced to them, is a law or not, or whether it is void, under an opinion that it is unconstitutional, that is, contrary to the Constitution of the United States. *** It is one thing to decide what the law is on the facts proved, and another and a very different thing, to determine that the statute produced is no law.

Francis Wharton, *State Trials of the United States During the Administrations of Washington and Adams*, 688, 710, 713 (Phil. 1849).

the Chief Justice also told them that "[t]he facts comprehended in the case, are agreed; the only point that remains, is to settle what is the law of the land arising from those facts." [42]

Moreover, the leading scholar on the history of the Supreme Court for that early period has responded: "But Justice Curtis would have been surprised if he had investigated further, for he would have found that the elements of *Brailsford* that he had questioned were indeed reported correctly by Dallas."[43] Furthermore, at the time of the *Morris* trial, there were plenty of other published authorities to the same effect, those cited by Hale but others not, more recent than *Brailsford* and pronounced by Supreme Court justices on circuit, including Chief Justice Marshall.[44]

It is important to identify precisely where Justice Curtis drew the line. He did not contend for the kind of special verdict that Lord Chief Justice Mansfield imposed in seditious libel cases and which Parliament overruled in Fox's Libel Act.[45] He defined the jury's powers this way:

---

[42] 3 U.S. at 4.

[43] Maeva Marcus, "Georgia v. Brailsford," 1996 *Journal of Supreme Court History*, Vol. II, 57. In the discussion of this case in *The Documentary History of the Supreme Court of the United States, 1789–1800* (8 vols. Columbia Univ. Press 1985-2007) Vol. VI, *Cases 1790–1795*, at 86 n. 78, the editors say: "Despite some scholarly comment to the contrary, Jay's discussion of the jury's power to find the law appears to be an accurate description of the state of affairs in the 1790s."

[44] See cases collected in John D. Gordan, III, "Juries as Judges of the Law: the American Experience," 108 L.Q.R. 272, 274–276 (1992). See also Stacy Pratt McDermott, *The Jury in Lincoln's America* (Ohio UP 2012), 144–161.

[45] See James Oldham, *English Common Law in the Age of Mansfield* (UNC 2004), 209–235. However, Justice Curtis misused the peculiarities of seditious libel to distinguish the case before him from *Croswell*, while disregarding the broader principle which Justice James Kent's opinion relied. He also pointed out that the court had been divided — Kent and Smith Thompson, a future U. S. Supreme Court, on one side, Morgan Lewis and Brockholst Livingston on the other — without acknowledging that when Livingston reached the U.S.

That it has been a familiar saying among the profession in this country, and an opinion entertained by highly respectable judges, that the jury are judges of the law as well as of the facts, I have no doubt. In some sense I believe it to be true, for they are the sole judges of the application of the law to that particular case. In this sense, theirs is the duty to pass on the law.... [B]ut it is not their province to decide any question of law in criminal, any more than civil cases; and if they should intentionally fail to apply to the case the law given to them by the Court, it would be, in my opinion, as much a violation of duty as if they were knowingly to return a verdict contrary to the evidence.

Justice Curtis's position was clearly against the weight of existing authority originating at the founding of the Republic and in the decades immediately thereafter.[46] He was supported by a relatively recent decision of Justice Story's,[47] but Story's

---

Supreme Court, on circuit he ruled the other way. *United States v. Hoxie*, 26 Fed. Cas. 397, 402–403 (No. 15,407) (C.C.D.Vt. 1808).

[46] See Jonathan Bressler, "Reconstruction and the Transformation of Jury Nullification," 78 *U. Chi. L. Rev.* 1133, 1138–1142 (2011); William E. Nelson, "The Lawfinding Power of Colonial American Juries," 71 *Ohio State L. Rev.* 1003 (2010); Mark DeWolfe Howe, "Juries as Judges of Criminal Law," 52 *Harv. L. Rev.* 582 (1939); see also the authorities cited in Gordan, *supra* page 67, n. 44. A comprehensive summary of the relevant authorities also appears in the Minority Report on the bill in favor of Susan B. Anthony authored by Matthew Hale Carpenter. Senate Report No. 472, 43d Congress, Ist Sess. (June 20, 1874). To these may be added Bingham v. Cabbot, 3 U.S. 19, 33 (1795). A related interesting but ultimately unpersuasive analysis appears in Laura I. Appleman, "The Lost Meaning of the Jury Trial Right," 84 *Indiana L. J.* 397 (2008).

[47] *United States v. Battiste*, 24 Fed. Cas. 1042 (No. 14,545) (C.C.D. Mass. 1835). The moral ambiguity of *Battiste* matches that of *Prigg*. Represented at trial by Daniel Webster and C. P. Curtis, Benjamin Robbins Curtis's cousin and then law partner, Battiste was a mate on an American vessel which took aboard and disembarked slaves at ports on the coast of Portuguese Africa, "with the exception of a little girl, taken in at Nova Redondo, who was afterwards brought by Captain Miller to New York," and who disappears into the darkness at that point. Battiste had been over-indicted for slave trading, a capital offense, and Justice

opinion was such a departure from existing precedent that
James Kent viewed it as a "monstrous heretical doctrine":

> My judicial opinion against such a Doctrine is to be seen in
> *Croswell's Case* in *3 Johnson's Cases*, in the Appendix. If
> the jury have nothing to do with *the law* on the plea of not
> guilty on Trials in capital cases, if whether the accused did
> the Act traitorously and feloniously, Be not a proper
> question for the Jury, then I think the boasted Trial by Jury
> evaporates in Smoke, & our English and American
> Ancestors were in gross Error in asserting with such
> vehemence the right to *Trial by Jury* as the Safety & Glory
> of the common law.[48]

Justice Curtis's decision denied Morris the protection of
what Lord Devlin rightly called "the conscience of the jury"
and the "jury as a safeguard against repugnant laws" and what
J. R. Pole, speaking of Justice James Wilson's lectures on law
in 1790 and 1791, described as "[t]he jury's moral agency," a
concept Pole found supported by *Brailsford* and *Croswell*.[49]
Justice Curtis was forthright about his justification for
requiring the jury to obey strictly the Court's instructions on
the law:

Story effectively charged that case out of court while asserting that
Battiste was guilty of a misdemeanor, to which he subsequently
pleaded guilty after his acquittal by the jury. Arguably, Justice Story
was sacrificing jury autonomy to protect the defendant from the
misconstruction of the statute by a vengeful jury.

[48] Daniel J. Hulsebosch, "Debating the Transformation of American
Law: James Kent, Joseph Story and the Legacy of the Revolution," in
Daniel W. Hamilton and Alfred L. Brophy (eds.), *Transformations in
American Legal History – Essays In Honour of Professor Morton J.
Horwitz* (Harvard Law School 2009), Vol. 1, 1, 18.

[49] P. Devlin, "The Conscience of the Jury," 187 L.Q.R. 398 (1991); *id.*,
Trial by Jury (The Hamlyn Lectures) (London 1956); J. R. Pole,
*Contract & Consent: Representation and the Jury in Anglo-American
Legal History*, 66, 80, 128–129 & n.22 (Virginia 2010). See also E. P.
Thompson, "The State versus its 'Enemies,'" in *Writing by candlelight*
(London 1980), 99, 108: "The jury attends in judgement, not only upon
the accused, but also upon the justice and humanity of the Law."

The sole end of courts of justice is to enforce the laws uniformly and impartially, without respect of persons or times, or the opinions of men. To enforce popular laws is easy. But when an unpopular cause is a just cause, when a law, unpopular in some locality, is to be enforced there, then comes the strain upon the administration of justice; and few unprejudiced men would hesitate as to where that strain would be most firmly borne.

And, as Dana's trial notes show, Justice Curtis's opening instructions to the jury after rendering his opinion followed this view: "Prelim. qu. is to powers of Ct & Jury — Jury must take the law as given by Ct. & the jury solely to apply the Cts [instructions] to the facts." However, having heard Hale, "in spite of the Court, the jury believed him, and acquitted his client."[50]

JUSTICE CURTIS'S CHARGE TO THE JURY[51]

Although his instructions on the elements of the crimes charged appear unexceptional, Dana's notes demonstrate that

---

[50] Horace Binney, *The Leaders of the Old Bar of Philadelphia*, 16 (1859)(speaking of Andrew Hamilton at the trial of John Peter Zenger).

[51] Regrettably, Justice Curtis's trial notebooks do not include notes of his jury charges. His charge in *Morris* is not reported. It exists in two versions. One is in the notes of the trial in Dana's *Morris* case file. The other is in Volume 2 of the Curtis Memoir, at 172–175. Although not so identified, the latter was taken word for word from the report of the charge in *The Commonwealth*. Not only does it omit a number of statements found in Dana's notes which are significant to a lawyer's eyes, it also contains a statement — "Even if it do [sic] not appear that he aided in the rescue, yet if he was present, and did nothing to prevent it, this would render him guilty under the statute," *id.* at 174 — an unbelievably prejudicial instruction that the Kendricks, supra n. 2 at 204, correctly characterize as "tantamount to an instruction to find Morris guilty as charged" but one which Dana's notes demonstrate that the newspaper reporter subtly misrecorded. Dana's notes, reproduced in the appendix to this paper, are therefore primarily relied on, with supplementation from the *Commonwealth* version where necessary.

Justice Curtis built on the mischief done by his two earlier opinions in what can only be seen as an effort to obtain Morris's conviction; the first is noted in the preceding paragraph, above.

On the issue of Shadrach's status as a slave, Justice Curtis charged the jury that the evidence given by De Bree and Caphart was prima facie evidence of that status. Then, according to Dana's notes, Justice Curtis "reads from opinion of Sup. Ct. in 6 Pet. [31 U.S. 622,] 632 *Kelly v. Jackson* [1832]," undoubtedly some part of this passage:

> What is *prima facie* evidence of a fact? It is such as, in judgment of law, is sufficient to establish the fact; and, if not rebutted, remains sufficient for the purpose. The jury are bound to consider it in that light, unless they are invested with authority to disregard the rules of evidence, by which the liberty and estate of every citizen are guarded and supported. *** In a legal sense, then, such *prima facie* evidence, in the absence of all controlling evidence, or discrediting circumstances, becomes conclusive of the fact; that is, it should operate on the minds of the jury as decisive to found their verdict as to the fact.

Curtis added: "*Conclusive of the fact*, it is *decisive*." In essence, having stripped Morris of the evidentiary presumption of Shadrach's freedom under Virginia law in his earlier opinion, Justice Curtis went further and directed the jury to treat the testimony of De Bree and Caphart as conclusive on the issue of Shadrach's being a slave. Judge Sprague had given the same instruction at both the *Scott* and *Hayden* trials.[52]

Moreover, in that context but also of more general application, Dana's notes record that Justice Curtis also charged the jury that unless the testimony of a witness were discredited, "the duty of the jury is to render their verdict in acc[ordance] with it" and that the "Jury [is] to believe a witness unless impeached" which could occur by reputation evidence, "the improbability of the story" or "his disclosed

---

[52] *The Commonwealth* June 6 and 17, 1851.

character." Dana's notes then immediately add "tempestuous sensibilities," which appear in this context in the *Commonwealth* report of Justice Curtis's charge as follows:

> Then as to Caphart. The law has provided rules; and one is that a witness under oath is to be believed, unless in some way his testimony is impeached or invalidated. Is there any thing adduced here going to impugn Caphart's character for truth and veracity? It has been argued that he has made such statements as to his relations with the colored population as should have that effect. A witness, a stranger among us, should be treated with fairness, and not be overwhelmed by our tempestuous sensibilities.

Although Justice Curtis did then inform the jury that if they disbelieved Caphart, they could not convict on the first thirteen counts pleaded under the Fugitive Slave Act, his earlier instructions left the jury little alternative than to credit Caphart's testimony and seem to have been given solely to counteract the impact of Hale's denunciation of Caphart. A rule that a witness under oath is to be believed unless impeached is not one found in modern jury instructions nor in fully reported federal trials preceding the Civil War. [53]

THE VERDICT

The jury went out on November 11 and reported its verdict of acquittal the next morning. Theodore Parker recorded in his journal:

> Hon. John P. Hale came in, all radiant and flushed with delight, to say that the jury had acquitted Morris. "Lord, now lettest thou thy servant depart in peace; for mine eyes have seen thy salvation." This is more than I expected. All

---

[53] Justice Curtis's instruction on this point may be contrasted with Justice Baldwin's in *Johnson v. Tompkins*, 13 Fed. Cas. 840, 850 (No. 7,416), (C.C. E.D. Pa. 1833) upon which his opinion relies for other purposes.

that Boston influence and the money of the United States could do—all that shameless impudence could do—has been done, and the jury acquit! Well, the jury is not yet to be despaired of, [in]spite of the judicial tyranny that seeks to unman them.[54]

Preoccupied, Dana's reaction, in his diary, was somewhat different. Thirty-six hours before Justice Curtis charged the jury, the pastor of Dana's church had suddenly collapsed at the end of the evening service and died a few minutes later at his home, a man Dana described in his diary as "my spiritual father, the guide of my children." After the verdict was rendered on the morning of November 12, Dana must have gone directly from the courthouse to the funeral, where, as he reported in his weekly diary entry on November 16:

There was scarcely a dry eye in the house. Men wept like children, & grasped each other's hands in silence, & women sobbed audibly.

On the 9th day of Nov. 1851, at evening... on the Lord's day, at the last words of the evening service, while kneeling, with his face to the altar, with the whole gospel armor on, in the white robes of his sacred office, the Angel touched him, "The Lord hath need of thee", & as the sun went down his spirit obeyed the summons. ***

He lived on & for & in the Church and its services, the poor, the sick, the afflicted & the penitent. He was one of the few, very few clergymen, who remained in Boston during the trying Cholera season, & when the ship fever prevailed, he went to Deer Island to bury utter strangers, poor emigrants, whose friends wanted the Church service, when no one else would go. ***

---

[54] John Weiss, *Life and Correspondence of Theodore Parker* (New York 1864), Vol. 2, 105.

> The other event, is the acquittal of Morris. I hope this will end the Rescue Cases. Judge Curtis' charge was lucid & absolutely impartial.[55]

Dana's comment on the charge must be evaluated in the context of the way Justice Curtis's earlier rulings had shaped the case for the jury. He had already substantially removed Shadrach's slave status as an obstacle to Morris's conviction by his evidentiary opinion, which Dana deplored. Similarly, his insistence that the jury accept his instructions on the law had the apology of the pursuit of an objective verdict on the facts consistent with — rather than in the teeth of — the elements of the Fugitive Slave Act. Thus confined by these prior rulings, the issues left to the jury depended on their evaluation of Morris's conduct and intent during a brief period on the afternoon of February 15, 1851, and, having prevailed on those issues, Dana could understandably have felt that Justice Curtis's "charge was lucid & absolutely impartial."[56]

What led to the jury's verdict is unknowable. The *Scott* jury had advised Judge Sprague that "the jury are united in the law as administered by the Court. They cannot agree upon the evidence," and the *Hayden* jury reported its deadlock in

---

[55] Dana Journal 467–469.

[56] This interpretation is consistent with the discussion of the *Morris* trial in the *Twentieth Annual Report Presented to the Massachusetts Anti-Slavery Society, supra,* page 31, n. 8, at 16:

> It is but due, however, to Mr. Justice Curtis, who presided at the trial, to say, that, setting aside his jury-catechising and his vindication of his monopoly of the law (in which he but followed the antipathies native to his species; for what great Judge was there ever that did not hate a Jury?) with these inconsiderable exceptions, his conduct during the trial was unexceptionable, and his charge impartial. His conduct in this particular honorably contrasted with that of Judge Sprague on the previous trials, who seemed to regard it as his mission to make good the forensic shortcomings of the poetical District Attorney.

similar terms.[57] In each case Judge Sprague's instructions had been emphatic that, as he put it at the *Scott* trial, "whether Shadrach was a slave or not, was of no consequence with regard to the last three counts of the indictment",[58] a concept also found in Justice Curtis's charge at the *Morris* trial. Since the juries at the earlier trials were unable to acquit or convict on any of the counts, a fair inference is that their disagreement involved more than Shadrach's slave status.

The only acquittal other than Morris's was Elizur Wright's, also at a second trial after a hung jury at the first. It is now well documented that one of the jurors at Wright's second trial, Francis Bigelow, had given Shadrach shelter at his home in Concord on the night of his escape and had driven him in a closed carriage to Leominster on the morning of February 16.[59]Although these facts did not emerge until the end of the nineteenth century, there certainly seems to have been an awareness at Wright's second trial that there was more to Francis Bigelow than met the eye. In his reminiscences published in 1903, long-time United States Senator from Massachusetts George F. Hoar reported:

> I went into the court-room during the trial of Mr. Wright and saw seated in the front row of the jury, wearing a face of intense gravity, my old friend Francis Bigelow, always spoken of in Concord as "Mr. Bigelow, the blacksmith." He was Free Soiler and his wife a Garrison Abolitionist. His house was a station on the underground railroad where fugitive slaves were harbored on their way to Canada. Shadrach had been put into a buggy and driven out as far as Concord, and kept over night by Bigelow at his house, and sent on his way toward the North Star the next morning. Richard H. Dana, who was counsel for Elizur Wright, asked Judge Hoar what sort of a man Bigelow was. To which the Judge replied: "He is a thoroughly honest man,

---

[57] *The Commonwealth* June 7 and 18, 1851. The newspaper reported that the *Scott* jury was evenly divided and the *Hayden* jury 9 to 3 for conviction.

[58] *The Commonwealth* June 7 and 18, 1851.

[59] Collison, *Shadrach Minkins, supra,* page xvii, n. 10, 151–162.

and will decide the case according to the law and the evidence as he believes them to be. But I think it will take a good deal of evidence to convince him that one man owns another."[60]

The lore of the Rescue cases has created phantom Bigelow-like "faithful jurors" at Rescue trials where the jury could not agree. Speaking of Wright's first trial, his biographer says: "One juror, who later admitted to being one of Shadrac[h]'s rescuers, blocked the guilty verdict of his eleven peers."[61] Dana noted in his diary on June 10, 1852, on hearing of its outcome:

> The jury disagreed in Elisur [sic] Wright's case. Eleven for conviction & one for acquittal. It seems as if Providence always raised up at last one faithful man on each jury to prevent a conviction in these cases.[62]

Building from that entry, in his biography of Dana, Charles Francis Adams recounts:

> Some year or more after the rescue trials were over, Dana had occasion to deliver a political speech in Middlesex County, not far from the New Hampshire state line. After the meeting had dissolved, and he was preparing to leave the hall, he was approached by a quiet, plain-looking man, who inquired if he remembered him. After looking at the man a moment, Dana answered, "Yes. You were the twelfth juror in ____'s case;" mentioning one of the rescue trials. The man immediately replied, "Yes; I was the twelfth juror in that case, and I was the man who drove Shadrach over the line."

---

[60] George F. Hoar, *Autobiography of Seventy Years* (2 vols. New York 1903), Vol. 1, 181–182. Judge Hoar was George Hoar's brother Ebenezer, lawyer, state court trial judge, Justice of the Massachusetts Supreme Judicial Court and Attorney General of the United States in the Grant administration.

[61]Goodheart, *supra,* page 30, n. 5, 136.

[62] Dana Journal 492.

"Now," Dana would add, "how singular it was that Lunt and the United States marshal should have raked the district of Massachusetts to find a jury that would convict in that case, and had subjected the whole panel to special investigation to establish the fact that no one in it had such a bias as would prevent conviction, ____ actually packing the jury ___, and yet succeeded in getting into the jury-box the one man who had been instrumental in running Shadrach out of the jurisdiction!"[63]

Given the role of Bigelow and his *doppelgangers* in these cases, it is surprising that no notice has been taken of the fact that the foreman of the *Morris* jury was named Stephen Kendall, and that Bearse's list of the some 200 members of the Vigilance Committee included Stephen B. Kendall.[64] The impanelling process did include a *voir dire* that had been crafted over defense objections at the earlier trials:

1. Have you formed or expressed any opinion in the matter now to be tried?

2. Are you sensible of any prejudice or bias therein?

***

4. Do you hold any opinions of the Fugitive Slave Law, so called, which will induce you to refuse to convict a person indicted under it, if the facts set forth in the indictment and constituting the offense are proved against him, and the Court direct you that the law is constitutional?

Justice Curtis's trial notes reflect the answers of each member of the venire panel to these questions. Stephen Kendall answered each of them "No" and was sworn.[65] Perhaps he was Dana's "one faithful man" at the *Morris* trial.

---

[63] Adams, *supra*, page 37, n. 21, 216–217.
[64] The names of the jurors are endorsed on the indictments in the Archives. Bearse, *supra*, page 44, n. 8, 4.
[65] Curtis Trial Notes 182.

CHAPTER V

Aftermath

THE WRIGHT TRIALS

Dana's hope was not to be realized: Morris's acquittal did not end the Rescue cases. There remained two trials, both of Elizur Wright, the defendant Webster wanted to convict, one in June, 1852, which ended in a hung jury and the other October, 1852 which ended in an acquittal. After defending at his first trial without counsel,[1] at the second he was represented by Dana and a new lead counsel, George Farley. These trials proceeded quickly, since, apart from the testimony of Shadrach's slave status, the Government's proof consisted of the testimony of two deputy marshals to whom Wright had been rude and obstreperous in the courtroom before the rescue and who claimed Wright had come in with the crowd as it broke into the courtroom, shouting "in, in!",

---

[1] There is no specific indication whether this was Wright's choice, particularly since Dana makes the point in his further discussion of Wright's near-conviction at his first trial that "[t]he general impression is that Wright might have been acquitted if he had counsel." Dana Journal 492. Dana seems to have been no admirer of Wright. In a letter to "the Misses Marsh," his wife's relatives, dated December 31, 1851, Dana wrote:

> As the "Commonwealth" has passed entirely into the hands of Wright, who is a curious fellow, rather an Ishmael, & our party is no longer responsible for it, & it is impossible to say what opinions he may advocate, I have not renewed the subscription for the coming year. I dare say you will miss it, but such sober minded Conservative persons as ourselves, of the old Federal stock, may forego the entertainments of a radical, half-Socialist, experimenter.
>
> (Dana Papers, Mass. Historical Society).

and of witnesses to an altercation Wright had had a few days before the rescue in connection with an election:

> [A]t the time referred to, Wright said to him, "I suppose you are one of those damned dough faces — Whigs — who, if a fugitive were pursued here, would help to arrest him." I said I hoped no such case would occur, but if it should, I would go with the law. "Then you are," said he, "just such a damned scoundrel as I took you to be, and if I should be there I should blow your brains out." He stated he would resist the law, and shoot any man who would attempt to enforce it.[2]

Robert Morris appeared as a defense witness at both trials, having been barred from the witness stand at his own by the rule of evidence precluding the accused's testimony. He testified that the crowd entered the courtroom as he left it with Charles G. Davis at his heels, and that from where Wright was standing in the courtroom he could not have reached the courtroom door to get outside before the crowd came in.[3] Despite the much stronger evidence against Morris at his own trial about his conduct in the street with Shadrach, Lunt attempted no cross examination on that score. Had he done so, he could have elicited from Morris an admission that he had been in the coach with Shadrach after all, having been partially thrust into it by the crowd when he approached those inside to remonstrate against their stealing it.[4]

Justice Curtis's jury instructions at the first trial do not survive, but Dana's notes of his charge at the second trial do and are reproduced in the appendix. The contrast between his jury instructions in *Morris* and eleven months later in *Wright* is striking. In *Wright*:

---

[2] *The Commonwealth*, June 7, 1852.

[3] Curtis Trial Notes, Vol. 2, 96–97 (first trial), 163–164 (second trial).

[4] Dana's *Morris* case file contains a document, seemingly in Morris's handwriting, similar to a brief to counsel, setting out his version of the facts and the expected testimony of potential witnesses for the defense, including Dana.

Elizur Wright
Photomechanical by unknown photographer, no date.
From Portraits of American Abolitionists. Photograph number 81.717.
Courtesy of the Massachusetts Historical Society

a.   he essentially charged the Government's pre-rescue courtroom proof out of the case, leaving to the jury only the issue of Wright's alleged conduct as the crowd was breaking in.

b.   far from directing that the jury must believe a witness in the absence of impeachment, he offered "[r]ules of experience as to judging facts" which emphasized reasonable doubt.

c.   while again specifying that Shadrach's slave status was irrelevant to the obstruction counts laid under the Act of 1790, Justice Curtis charged that on the Fugitive

Slave Act counts it must be proved that Shadrach was a slave under the law of Virginia and that:

1. the rules of evidence for this case are the Common Law, not the rules of Virginia, and the Common Law presumes that all men are free; and being held and treated as a slave is evidence of slavery, but does not constitute slavery. [5]

On Sunday October 24, 1852, in the midst of Wright's second trial Daniel Webster died. Justice Curtis's brother, George Ticknor Curtis, had been with Webster at the execution of his will on his deathbed on the evening of October 21 and testified at Wright's trial the following afternoon.[6] When Curtis charged the *Wright* jury on October 26, he knew he would not have to answer to Webster for the outcome.

THE RENDITION OF ANTHONY BURNS IN MAY–JUNE 1854

In many ways this was a re-rerun of the Shadrach rescue, except that the rescue failed. Burns was arrested on the night of May 24 and taken the next morning before a U. S. Commissioner under the Fugitive Slave Act, Edward G. Loring, who was also a lecturer at Harvard Law School, a state probate judge and a step-brother of Benjamin Robbins Curtis's father-in-law. Dana and Robert Morris, accompanied by Wendell Phillips and Rev. Theodore Parker, met Burns there

---

[5] Notwithstanding the radical change in Justice Curtis's attitude, Dana was cranky. He wrote a query — valid in law but strange under the circumstances — under the last of Curtis's instructions, asking what were the facts that did have to be proved. In addition, after two days of trial he wrote an extended note to his diary, complaining about a deficiency in one of the *voir dire* questions, which Justice Curtis recognized but did not remedy for want of a proposed alternative, and about Justice Curtis having interrupted his opening for venturing too far from the facts of the case. Dana Journal 511–512.

[6] Webster Papers 365–372; *The Commonwealth*, October 26, 1852.

Theodore Parker
Courtesy of the Boston Athanaeum

and persuaded Loring to adjourn the case for two days, until May 27; Loring remanded Burns to the custody of the marshal.

The Vigilance Committee began planning his rescue, the attempt providing the climax to a tumultuous meeting on the evening of May 26 at Faneuil Hall, where dramatic speeches by Phillips and then Parker whipped the crowd into a frenzy, and a prearranged signal sent them off to the courthouse, christened "the fortified slave pen," where Burns was being held. The rescuers, Lewis Hayden in the lead, were able to knock one of the courthouse doors off its hinges, but there was shooting, one of the marshal's guard was stabbed to death, the city police intervened, and the crowd retreated empty handed. Troops were ordered out and took possession of the courthouse square.

On May 27, after a further brief hearing, Commissioner Loring granted the defense request for a further adjournment to May 29. The Rev. Theodore Parker made use of the intervening Sunday to deliver a sermon in which he took a swipe at George Ticknor Curtis for cowardice — "The old fugitive slave bill Commissioner stands back; he has gone to look after his 'personal popularity'. But when Commissioner Curtis does not appear in this matter, another man comes forward...," Edward Greeley Loring. Having praised Loring for his humanity, respectability and charity, Parker denounced him as culpable in the death of the member of the marshal's guard, "your fellow servant in kidnapping."

The hearing before Commissioner Loring resumed on May 29 and lasted until May 31. On Friday June 2 Commissioner Loring gave judgment for Burns's claimant, and that afternoon, as Sims had been three years before, Burns was marched by United States Marines backed by artillery to the waterfront and put on a vessel to return to slavery in Alexandria, Virginia.[7]

The following Wednesday Justice Benjamin Robbins Curtis delivered a charge to a newly-empanelled grand jury in the circuit court, devoting considerable discussion to Section 22 of the Crimes Act of 1790 and focusing on the liability as principals of those who encouraged illegal conduct without actual participation — again a shot across the bows of Parker and Phillips and their associates. However, the grand jury returned no indictments. On October 16 a new grand jury was empanelled, one of its members being Justice Benjamin Robbins Curtis's brother-in-law William Greenough. At Justice Curtis's direction, Benjamin F. Hallett, who had succeeded Lunt as United States district attorney in 1853, provided the grand jurors with Justice Curtis's June 7 grand jury charge, and indictments were returned against Theodore

---

[7] Earl M. Maltz, *Fugitive Slave on Trial: The Anthony Burns Case and Abolitionist Outrage* (Kansas 2010). Von Frank, *supra*, p. xvii, n. 11; Henry Steele Commager, *Theodore Parker* (Boston 1947), 231–242; Charles Emery Stevens, *Anthony Burns: A History* (Boston 1856); *The Boston Slave Riot, and Trial of Anthony Burns* (Boston 1854).

Parker, Wendell Phillips and others involved at the Faneuil Hall rally and attempted break-in at the courthouse on May 26.[8] Hallett had taken the hint first given by Judge Sprague and then by Justice Curtis at each of the Shadrach Rescue trials and which Justice Curtis had emphasized in his charge to the Grand Jury on June 7: the slave status of a fugitive was not an element of the offense of obstructing the execution of process by the marshal under Section 22 of the Crimes Act of 1790. Thus, Hallett took that issue out of the indictments for the attempted rescue of Burns by limiting them to five counts laid under Section 22; no charges were brought, as they been in the Shadrach Rescue cases, under the Fugitive Slave Act of 1850.[9]

Parker was arrested and arraigned on November 29 and posted bond. Trial was first set for March and then postponed to April 3, 1855. After the event, Parker wrote that he was certain that, because "there were facts, sure to come to light, not honorable to the Court and not pleasant to look at in the presence of a New England community then getting indignant at the outrages of the Slave Power," the judges would never let the case "come to the jury":

> At the "trial," April 3d, it was optional with the defendant's counsel to beat the Government on the indictment before the

---

[8] Charge to the Grand Jury, 30 F. Cas. 983 (No. 18,250) (C.C.D. Mass. 1854); 2 Curtis's Circuit Court Reports 637; Parker Trial, ix–xvii, 170–180. Apart from the useful reproduction of court documents associated with this abortive prosecution, the Parker Trial is a engrossing 200-page mixture of history, law and diatribe in the form of a summation that Parker would never have been allowed to embark on at a trial that never took place. Its substance appears to have been inspired by Charles Sumner, who wrote to Parker on January 9, 1855 from the floor of the U.S. Senate: "Of course, *you must* speak for yourself before Pontius Pilate [Curtis]. I think you should make the closing speech, and review the whole movement in Boston, which culminated in your indictment, and arraign its intent and action — of course touching upon the courts." B.W. Palmer (ed.), *The Selected Letters of Charles Sumner* (Northeastern 1990), Vol. 1, 424.

[9] Parker's indictment is reproduced in full at Parker Trial xiii–xvii.

Wendell Phillips
Courtesy of the Boston Athanaeum

Court; or on the merits of the case before the Jury. ***
[O]n the whole, it was thought best to blow up the enemy
in his own fortress and with his own magazine, rather than
to cut him to pieces with our shot in the open field.[10]

---

[10] *Id.* at vi–vii. Previously, Justice Curtis had written somewhat self-
consciously to his uncle George Ticknor on December 20, 1854:

> I suppose great efforts are making, and will continue to be made, to
> preoccupy the public mind with reference to the trials of Theodore
> Parker and Wendell Phillips. This is no affair of mine. My duty is to
> administer the law. This will be done. Whether they are legally guilty
> of the charge, whether either of them ought to be convicted, whether
> they will be convicted are matters respecting which I have no
> responsibility whatever, and, I can say with perfect truth, no wish
> whatever save that justice should be done.

Curtis Memoir, Vol. 2, 175.

On that day, Parker's counsel, the ever-faithful John P. Hale, still a United States Senator, with counsel for the other six defendants named in separate indictments, proposed to file a joint motion to dismiss applicable to all cases, which was accepted.[11] The fourth ground of the motion was the following:

> 4. Because the said indictment does not allege and set forth fully and sufficiently the authority and the proceedings whereon the alleged warrant and order were based, or facts sufficient to show that the alleged process and order were lawfully issued by any person duly authorized, and his authority and jurisdiction, and that the same were within such jurisdiction, and issued by the authority of the law, and originated, issued and directed as the law prescribes; said warrant and order not being alleged to have been issued from any court or tribunal of general or special jurisdiction, but by a person issued with certain specific statute authority.

After several days of argument by other counsel and the Government, Justice Curtis stopped Hale from replying, on the grounds that the indictment was fatally defective because its averment that Loring was a Commissioner of the Circuit Court of the United States for the District of Massachusetts insufficiently alleged that he was a Commissioner under the Fugitive Slave Act, under which the warrant of arrest and order of remand had been issued.[12] All of the indictments were dismissed or nol prossed.

---

[11] The full text of the motion is set out at Parker Trial xviii.

[12] Parker Trial xix. *United States v. Stowell*, 27 F. Cas. 1350 (No. 16,409) (C.C.D. Mass. 1855). Specifically, Justice Curtis's lengthy opinion, relying solely on British pleading precedents, turned on his identification of a federal statute enacted in 1848 which created a species of commissioner appointed for extraditions but not empowered to issue a fugitive slave warrant, and thus "[t]he averment that the person who issued this warrant, was a commissioner appointed by the circuit court, would be fully satisfied by proof, that he was appointed to make extradition under treaties, though he had no other power whatever … to issue this warrant." Justice Curtis held that the fact that the indictment named Loring as the commissioner, that he did have

In 1879, twenty-five years after these events, nearly twenty years after Parker's death and five years after Curtis's, the cool dispassion expressed in his letter to his uncle before the trial had dissipated among his survivors. Denouncing Parker's *The Trial of Theodore Parker* as "one of the foulest libels that ever emanated from the press… against a judge whose legal acumen saved him from a trial", in the Curtis Memoir his brother George Ticknor Curtis said of this distinguished divine:

> He did a worse thing than this; for in his Preface he attributed his escape from a trial to his counsel, who, he said, "rent the indictment into many pieces – apparently to the great comfort of the judges, who thus escaped the battle, which then fell only on the head of the [U. S. District] Attorney." The indictment was quashed on an error detected and pointed out by the court, which had not been seen or referred to by the counsel for the defence. Mr. Parker knew this, of course, just as well as it was known to every one present.[13]

It is hard to perceive whether the ground for the Court's ruling is embraced in paragraph 4 of the motion. But the heat of the claim that Justice Curtis was its originator carries with it the strong implication that this was the position, not only of his brother, but also of Justice Curtis himself.

If that is so, then one must ask why Robert Morris and Elizur Wright were denied the benefit of that "legal acumen"

---

authority under the Fugitive Slave Act to issue the warrant, and that the indictment alleged it had been "duly" issued did not cure the pleading deficiency. *See* David R. Maginnes, "The Case of the Court House Rioters in the Rendition of the Fugitive Slave Anthony Burns, 1854," *Journal of Negro History* (January 1971), Vol. 56, 31.

[13] Curtis Memoir, Vol. 1, 177–178 & n.1. In contrast, in his Journal, Parker attributes the following comments on the hearing to his other counsel in the case, C.M Ellis: After five days of argument "[t]he judge showed *himself* out, and the temper of those he stood with. They sneaked off through the smallest place possible, but showed temper; needlessly declared that the jury was well drawn, and slurred at the counsel." Weiss, *supra*, page 73, n. 54, 146–148.

at their trials three-and-a-half years earlier. Counts 14–16 of their superseding indictments, which Justice Curtis submitted to one trial jury in Morris's case and to two in Wright's, suffered from exactly the same pleading deficiency as all the counts in Parker's. Nor were issues of the Fugitive Slave Act Commissioner's status wholly unexplored in those cases; at his first trial, the *pro se*:

> Mr. Wright moved that the Court would quash the indictment on account of the want of authority in the Commissioner before whom the proceedings against Shadrach were had. Mr. Commissioner Curtis testified he had no commission. The Constitution of the United States requires in the most positive manner that every officer shall have a commission. [14]

Even if that were not the case, Justice Curtis was sensitive to the status of a commissioner under the Act, since much of his opinion letter of November 9, 1850 sustaining its constitutionality centered on an analysis of the role of the commissioner under the Act and the limited nature of proceedings before commissioners generally in justifying the absence of a jury trial in rendition proceedings. [15]

The aftermath of the dismissals was even stranger than the dismissals themselves. Presumably to cure by superseding indictments what must have appeared to be a hypertechnical pleading deficiency, if that, Hallett requested the Court to recall the grand jury that had returned the original indictments, but the Court apparently objected because the marshal was not "an indifferent person", presumably because he was the alleged victim of the obstruction which was the subject of the indictments — a circumstance of which the Court was well aware when the Grand Jury had been originally impanelled. In addition, according to a letter from

---

[14] *The Commonwealth,* June 8, 1852.

[15] See, *supra,* page 16 & n.8.

13. And the jurors aforesaid, on their oath aforesaid do further present, that on the first day of June, in the year of our Lord one thousand eight hundred and fifty, a certain person of color, named Shadrach, and otherwise called Frederic Minkins, was a person lawfully held to service and labor in the state of Virginia, one of the said United States, under the laws of said Virginia, and owed said service and labor to one John DeBree, of Norfolk in said State, and the said Shadrach, otherwise called Frederick Minkins, while so held to service and labor in said state, and while owing such service and labor to said DeBree, did escape and flee from said service and labor, and from and out of said state of Virginia, to and into the Commonwealth of Massachusetts, another of said United States, and in the District aforesaid, and became and was a fugitive therein from said service and labor, and the said John DeBree to whom, as aforesaid, said service and labor was due, did afterwards, to wit, on the fourteenth day of February, eighteen hundred and fifty one, by one John Caphart, his agent and attorney, who was duly authorized in this behalf by said DeBree, by a power of attorney in writing by him legally executed, and acknowledged at Norfolk City, in said state of Virginia, on the eleventh day of February, eighteen hundred and fifty one, and duly certified under the seal of Richard H. Baker, Esquire, who then and there was judge of the Circuit Court of said city of Norfolk, and a legal officer of the said State of Virginia, pursue and reclaim said Shadrach, otherwise called Frederic Minkins, then a fugitive as aforesaid, in said Massachusetts, by said Caphart, whom on the fourteenth day of February aforesaid, and in pursuance of the said power and for the purpose of such pursuit, and reclamation, did make, file, and institute a complaint in due form of Law against said Shadrach, (otherwise called Frederic Minkins,) by his said name of Shadrach, for escaping from said service and labor, before George T. Curtis, Esquire, then a Commissioner of the Circuit Court of the United States, for said District, legally appointed within the district aforesaid, and did obtain from the said Commissioner, a warrant thereon in due form of law, the said District of Massachusetts being the proper District for the issuing thereof, and by which it was commanded to the Marshal of the United States for said District, or his Deputies, that they or one of them, should apprehend the said Shadrach, (otherwise called Frederic Minkins,) denominated in said warrant by his said name of Shadrach, and have him forthwith before said Commissioner, to be dealt with according to law, the said Commissioner being then and there duly qualified and authorised by law to receive said complaint and to issue said warrant, and said Caphart did on the fifteenth day of February aforesaid, deliver the said warrant for service to Patrick Riley, then and ever since one of the deputies of Charles Devens, Esq., and ever since has been, and still is the Marshal of the United States, for said District, and the said Riley by virtue of said warrant did on the said fifteenth day of February, eighteen hundred and fifty one, apprehend the said Shadrach otherwise called Frederic Minkins, and did take him before the said Commissioner as directed in, and by said warrant, and the said Commissioner did then at the request of the said Shadrach otherwise called Frederic Minkins, adjourn the hearing of the case upon said complaint, and did lawfully order the said Riley to retain the said Shadrach otherwise called Frederic Minkins, by his said name of Shadrach in his custody to have him before the said Commissioner on the eighteenth day of said February, at ten of the clock in the forenoon, for the further hearing of said complaint, and said Riley thereupon, and by virtue of said warrant and said order, did take and retain in his custody the said Shadrach otherwise called Frederic Minkins, for the purposes therein and thereby directed, and thereby and by means of the premises said Riley became and was a person lawfully assisting the said DeBree, and lawfully assisting the said Caphart the agent and attorney of the said DeBree, in pursuing and reclaiming the said Shadrach, otherwise called Frederic Minkins, then and there, a fugitive as aforesaid.

And the jurors, aforesaid, on their oath aforesaid, aver that after the passing the said order by the said Commissioner, and during the said fifteenth day of February, and while the said DeBree and his said agent and attorney Caphart were thus pursuing and reclaiming the said Shadrach otherwise called Frederic Minkins fugitive as aforesaid, and while he was so held and retained by the said Riley as aforesaid, one *Robert Morris of Chelsea in said* of the City of Boston, *in said District, Esquire,* with force and arms, at said Boston in said District, did knowingly, willingly, wilfully and unlawfully aid, abet and assist the said Shadrach, otherwise called Frederic Minkins, to escape from the said Riley, and from the said DeBree, and from the said Caphart the agent and attorney of the said DeBree, as aforesaid; and by means of such aid and assistance the said Shadrach otherwise called Frederic Minkins, did make his escape from the said Riley and from the said DeBree, and from the said Caphart.

Against the peace and dignity of the said United States, and contrary to the form of the Statute in such case made and provided.

14. And the Jurors aforesaid, on their oath aforesaid, do further present that on the fifteenth day of February, in the year of our Lord one thousand eight hundred and fifty-one, at Boston, in said District, the said *Robert Morris of Chelsea in said District Esquire* with force and arms, did knowingly and wilfully obstruct, resist and oppose one Patrick Riley, a deputy of Charles Devens, junior, Marshal of the United States for the District of Massachusetts, and an officer of the United States, in serving and attempting to serve and execute a certain warrant and legal process, which before that time, to wit, on the fourteenth day of February, in the year of our Lord one thousand eight hundred and fifty-one, had been duly issued under the hand and seal of George T. Curtis, Esquire, a Commissioner of the Circuit Court of the United States for Massachusetts District, and directed to the Marshal of our District of Massachusetts, or either of his Deputies which the said Riley, in the due and lawful execution of his said office, had then and there, in his hands and possession, for service of the same, and which he was then and there serving, and attempting to serve and execute; which warrant commanded the said Riley to apprehend one Shadrach, and to have him forthwith before the said Commissioner, then and there to be dealt with according to law;

Against the peace and dignity of the said United States, and contrary to the form of the statute in such case made and provided.

15. And the Jurors aforesaid, on their oath aforesaid do further present that on the fifteenth day of February, in the year of our Lord one thousand eight hundred and fifty-one, at Boston, in said District, the said *Robert Morris of Chelsea in said District* with force and arms, did knowingly and wilfully obstruct, resist and oppose one Patrick Riley, a deputy of Charles Devens, junior, Marshal of the United States for the District of Massachusetts, and an officer of the United States, in serving and attempting to serve and execute a certain legal process, which before that time, to wit, on the said fifteenth day of February, had been duly issued, under the hand of George T. Curtis, Esquire, Commissioner of the Circuit Court of the United States for the District of Massachusetts, and duly committed for obedience and execution to said Riley, wherein and whereby, and in pursuance of the command whereof, the said Riley was then and there, lawfully retaining, detaining, and holding one Shadrach, for the further hearing and determination of a certain complaint, upon which a warrant before that time, to wit on the fourteenth day of said February had been duly issued under the hand and seal of said Commissioner; by force of which warrant the said Shadrach, had been duly arrested and apprehended by the said Riley, and in execution of the same, on the said fifteenth day of day of February, had been brought by said Riley, before the said Commissioner;

Against the peace and dignity of the said United States and contrary to the form of the Statute in such case made and provided.

16. And the jurors aforesaid, on their oath aforesaid do further present that on the fifteenth day of February, in the year of our Lord one thousand eight hundred and fifty one, at Boston, in said District, the said *Robert Morris of Chelsea in said District* with force and arms did knowingly and wilfully obstruct, resist and oppose one Patrick Riley, a deputy of Charles Devens, junior, Marshal of the United States, for the District of Massachusetts, and an officer of the United States, in serving and attempting to serve and execute a certain warrant and legal process, which before that time, to wit, on the fourteenth day of February, in the year of our Lord one thousand eight hundred and fifty one had been duly issued under the hand and seal of George T. Curtis, Esq. a Commissioner of the Circuit Court of the United States, for Massachusetts District, and directed to the Marshal of our District of Massachusetts, or either of his deputies, which the said Riley, in the due and lawful execution of his said office, had then and there, in his hands and possession for service of the same and which he was then and there, serving and attempting to serve and execute; which warrant commanded the said Riley to apprehend one Shadrach, and to have him forthwith before the said Commissioner, then and there to be dealt with according to law; and in serving and attempting to serve and execute a certain further legal process, which before that time, to wit, on the said fifteenth day of February had been duly issued under the hand of said Commissioner, and duly committed for obedience and execution to the said Riley, wherein and whereby and in pursuance of the command whereof, the said Riley was then and there, lawfully retaining, detaining and holding the said Shadrach, for the further hearing and determination of a certain complaint upon which the warrant aforesaid had been issued by said Commissioner.

Excerpt from Robert Morris Indictment
(National Archives, Waltham, MA)

And the Jurors aforesaid do further present, that on the twenty-sixth day of May, in the year aforesaid, in pursuance of the warrant and legal process aforesaid, and of said further legal process and order last mentioned, the said Watson Freeman, Marshal as aforesaid, then and there, at the said Court House in said Boston, had in his custody the person of the said Anthony Burns, in the due and lawful execution of the said warrant and legal process, and of the said further legal process and order, in manner and form as he was therein commanded — and one Theodore Parker, of Boston, in said District, Clerk, then and there well knowing the premises, with force and arms did knowingly and wilfully obstruct, resist, and oppose the said Watson Freeman, then and there being an officer of the said United States, to wit, Marshal of the said District, in serving and attempting to serve and execute the said warrant and legal process, and the said further legal process and order in manner and form as he was therein commanded, to the great damage of the said Watson Freeman, to the great hinderance and obstruction of Justice, to the evil example of all others, in like case offending, against the peace and dignity of the said United States, and contrary to the form of the Statute in such case made and provided.

2d. And the Jurors aforesaid, on their oath aforesaid, do further present, that on the twenty-sixth day of May, in the year of our Lord one thousand eight hundred and fifty-four, at Boston, in said District, one Theodore Parker, of Boston, in said District, Clerk, with force and arms, did knowingly and wilfully obstruct, resist, and oppose one Watson Freeman, who was then and there the Marshal of the United States of America, for the District of Massachusetts, and an officer of the said United States, in serving and attempting to serve and execute a certain warrant and legal process, which before that time, to wit, on the twenty-fourth day of May, in the year of our Lord one thousand eight hundred and fifty-four, had been duly issued under the hand and seal of Edward G. Loring, Esquire, a Commissioner of the Circuit Court of the United States, for said District of Massachusetts, and directed to the Marshal of the District of Massachusetts, or either of his deputies, which said warrant and legal process the said Freeman, in the due and lawful execution of his said office, had then and there in his hands and possession for service of the same, and which he was then and there serving and attempting to serve and execute ; which said warrant commanded the said Freeman to apprehend one Anthony Burns and to have him forthwith before the said Commissioner, then and there to be dealt with according to law.   Against the peace and dignity of the said United States, and contrary to the form of the Statute in such case made and provided.

3d. And the Jurors aforesaid, on their oath aforesaid, do further present, that on the twenty-sixth day of May, in the year of our Lord one thousand eight hundred and fifty-four, at Boston, in said District, the said Theodore Parker, with force and arms, did knowingly and wilfully obstruct, resist, and oppose one Watson Freeman, who was then and there an officer of the said United States, to wit, the Marshal of the United States for the said District of Massachusetts, in serving and attempting to serve and execute a certain legal process which before that time, to wit, on the 25th day of May, in the year of our Lord one thousand eight hundred and fifty-four, had been duly issued under the hand of Edward G. Loring, who was then and there a Commissioner of the Circuit Court of the United States, for the said District of Massachusetts, and

Excerpt from Theodore Parker Indictment
(Parker Trial)

91

Hallett to President Franklin Pierce dated June 9, 1855, Justice Curtis was of the view, concurred in by Judge Sprague, that the failure to specify the commissioner's authority under the Fugitive Slave Act was a defect which infected not merely the indictment but also the warrant itself and the complaint on which the warrant had issued:

> Had the Indictment therefore enlarged this description it would have been of no avail. The difficulty is therefore inherent, and the result is that no Indictment could be sustained...[16]

Once again Justice Curtis relied on a purported deficiency which had given him no pause in 1851 Shadrach Rescue cases, counts in the indictments in which were based on a warrant with identical language issued by his brother. And on top of what must have seemed hypertechnical judicial attitudes, for the part he was playing Hallett had already been subject to censure by his colleagues at the bar. According to a note in Dana's diary dated March 30, 1855, just before argument on the motion to dismiss:

> Ned Sohier...met Hallett & asked him how he got along with his treason cases — (the cases ag. Theodore Parker, Phillips &c.). Hallett said he was getting on well eno,' but they abused him shockingly. "What do they say of you ?" said Sohier.
> "Why, they compare me with Judas Iscariot," said Hallett, "but *I don't mind that.*"
>
> "No!" said Sohier, "I should not think *you would*, but what would Judas say about it?"[17]

It seems that Justice Curtis had also concluded that there was nothing to be gained by having a trial. None of the

---

[16] Stanley W. Campbell, *The Slave Catchers: Enforcement of the Fugitive Slave Law, 1850-1860* (UNC 1970), 131–132, quoting Hallett to President Pierce, June 9, 1855. The warrant is reproduced in the Parker Trial at xiii–xiv as pleaded in the indictment.
[17] Dana Journal 674.

Shadrach Rescue trials had ended in a conviction. Rescue prosecutions around the nation since then had almost never succeeded.[18] On the other hand, the enforceability of the Fugitive Slave Act in Boston had been established by the *Sims*

---

[18] A somewhat inaccurate appendix in Campbell, *supra* n. 16, at 199-207, identifies the rescues of 22 slaves out of a total of 332 fugitive slave cases during the period 1850-1860, the largest number falling in 1851, and the earliest of these the rescue of Shadrach Minkins. The prosecutions for the two other rescues in 1851 were hardly more successful than those of Shadrach's rescuers.

The rescue of two slaves from a deputy marshal who was in the process of arresting them in September 1851 in Christiana, PA, led to violence that left their purported owner dead and an overreaching indictment of thirty-eight defendants for treason. At the conclusion of the first trial, which began on November 24, 1851 in the United States Circuit Court for the Eastern District of Pennsylvania, Circuit Justice Robert Grier instructed the jury that the proof did not show treason, and the remaining indictments were dismissed. *Trial of Castner Hanway for Treason in the Resistance of the Execution of the Fugitive Slave Law* (Philadelphia 1850); Thomas P. Slaughter, *Bloody Dawn:The Christiana Riot and Racial Violence in the Antebellum North* (Oxford 1991).

Similarly, the rescue in Syracuse of a slave named Jerry McHenry from the marshal's custody in October 1851 led to the indictment of twenty-six people. However, at trial in January 1853 only one was convicted — and died while the case was on appeal — one was acquitted, two had hung juries and the charges against the rest were dropped; the deputy marshal who had arrested the slave was prosecuted — but acquitted — in the New York State Courts for kidnapping. *Trial of Henry W. Allen, Deputy United States Marshal, for Kidnapping* (Syracuse 1852). Jayme A. Sokolow, "The Jerry McHenry Rescue and the Growth of Northern Antislavery Sentiment during the 1850s," *American Studies* (1982), Vol. 16, 427, 437 n. 28.

It was not until November 1854 that the first of two rescuers convicted for rescuing Joshua Glover was tried, and the convictions of both were embroiled in the Wisconsin Supreme Court by April 1855, when the *Burns* defendants were scheduled for trial. Baker, *supra,* page xvii, n. 11. Two later rescue prosecutions were more successful. *Report of the Trial of John Hossack Indicted for Rescuing a Fugivitive Slave from the U.S. Deputy Marshal at Ottawa, October 20th, 1859* (Chicago 1860); John J. Shipherd, *History of the Oberlin-Wellington Rescue* (Boston 1859); William Cheek and Aimee Lee Cheek, *John Mercer Langston and the Fight for Black Freedom 1829-65* (Illinois 1996).

rendition in 1851[19] and confirmed by the recent rendition of Burns, the attempted rescue of whom was the underlying basis for the indictments Justice Curtis dismissed.

Moreover, Hallett — although he too had attended Harvard Law School, in 1819 — had crossed a major boundary with this indictment. The Shadrach Rescue defendants had in the main been black, some prominent in their community, but, after the preliminary hearings, the only white defendant was Elizur Wright. The Burns Rescue defendants, on the other hand, included Boston's most prominent abolitionists, Wendell Phillips and Rev. Theodore Parker, as well as the Rev. Thomas W. Higginson, a Unitarian minister who had entered Harvard at the age of thirteen and graduated at the age of seventeen Phi Beta Kappa. It may be reading more precision into the words that George Ticknor Curtis used than he intended, in describing the Shadrach indictments, but what he said was:

> The Executive Government of the United States was brought face to face with the issue, whether a law of the United States should be executed in Massachusetts, or whether men of education and social position, who chose to be demagogues on this subject, should be permitted to stir up a spirit of open resistance to a statute, *without at least seeing their deluded and ignorant instruments brought to punishment.*[20]

Here Hallett had gone beyond the latter group and proposed to prosecute the "men of education and social position" themselves.

Curtis had wearied of Massachusetts abolitionist politics, as he wrote to his uncle, George Ticknor, from Washington in December 1854:

---

[19] See, *supra*, pp. 34–35.
[20] George Ticknor Curtis, *Life of Daniel Webster* (2 vols. New York 1870), Vol. 2, 489–490 (emphasis supplied).

I have not taken in a Boston newspaper this winter. I thought it more comfortable to leave Massachusetts behind me for three months…

It cannot be doubted that the position of the judges of the Supreme Court, at this time, is in a high degree onerous; and that it exposes them to attack, such as no honest judiciary, in any country, within my knowledge, have been subjected to, they have not the consideration and support to which they are entitled. The people… are ready to listen without indignation to the grossest charges against those who administer the judicial power. ***

[I]t has been a matter of grave doubt with me, whether I will longer continue to occupy the post I now hold. I can say with entire sincerity, that, if I could see an honorable retreat from my post open to me, from which the country would take no detriment, I would not hold it longer. [21]

Senator Hoar also suggests that by the time of the Burns Rescue prosecutions in 1855, Justice Curtis "probably got pretty sick of the whole thing."[22] Prior to the April 3, 1855 trial, abolitionist pressure had already cost Charles G. Loring his position as a lecturer at Harvard Law School, despite the anonymous support of George Ticknor Curtis, [23] and proceedings instigated by the abolitionists in the Massachusetts legislature for the removal by address of Judge Loring from his position as Judge of Probate because of his service as commissioner in the rendition of Anthony Burns were already under way. Wendell Phillips, one of the defendants before Justice Curtis, had testified in support of the removal on February 20, and Richard Henry Dana, Jr., although the losing counsel, had testified on March 5 in opposition to the removal; Dana considered that Loring had done no legal wrong in the *Burns* proceeding and quoted from

---

[21] Curtis Memoir, Vol. 1, 174–176.

[22] Hoar, *supra*, page 76, n. 60, 182.

[23] Paul Finkelman, "Legal Ethics and Fugitive Slaves: The Anthony Burns Case, Judge Loring and Abolitionist Attorneys," 17 *Cardozo L. Rev.* 1793, 1846–1852 (1996).

his contemporaneous diary entry, perhaps not with the effect he intended:

> The conduct of Judge Loring has been considerate and humane. If a man is willing to execute the law, and be an instrument of sending back a man into slavery under such a law, he could not act better in his office than Judge Loring.[24]

But if the political climate influenced Justice Curtis's action in the Burns Rescue cases, it did not prove to be for the better. As noted, armed with the dismissal, later in 1855 Rev. Theodore Parker put out a more than 200-page book containing a speech he purportedly intended to give to the jury at this trial before Justice Curtis. He was unsparing of the entire Curtis family, devoting over twenty pages to them as a group, and singling out Justice Curtis as a "man of superior understanding, and uncommon industry" but "apparently destitute of any high moral instincts." Towards the end of his denunciation of the Fugitive Slave Act, Parker said:

> You know who did all this: a single family—the Honorable Judge Curtis, with his kinsfolk and his friends, himself most subtly active with all his force throughout this work. When Mr. Webster prostituted himself to the Slave Power this family went out and pimped for him in the streets; they paraded in the newspapers, at the Revere House, and in public letters; they beckoned and made signs at Faneuil Hall. That crime of Sodom brought Daniel Webster to his grave at

---

[24] *Remarks of Richard H. Dana, Jr., Esq. before the Committee on Federal Relations on the Proposed Removal of Edward G. Loring from the Office of Judge of Probate, March 5, 1855* (Boston 1855), 17. This pamphlet, one containing Phillips's earlier testimony, and a number of other documents concerning the proceeding, which concluded in Loring's removal in 1858, are reproduced in P. Finkelman, ed., *Fugitive Slaves and American Courts*, Ser. II, Vol. III (New York 1988). Dana's position may explain why he was not counsel for one of the defendants in the *Burns* prosecutions, and the balance of the diary entry contemporaneous with his testimony before the legislature reflects his unhappiness with Loring's conduct. (Dana Journal 672).

Marshfield, a mighty warning not to despise the Law of the Infinite God; but that sin of Gomorrah, it put the Hon. Benj. R. Curtis on this Bench; gave him his judicial power to construct his "law," construct his "jury" to indict and try me.[25]

Parker did not spare George Ticknor Curtis, also a lawyer of great ability and versatility and the author of several significant legal treatises on such diverse subjects as merchant seamen, federal jurisdiction and copyright.[26] When the curtain rose in 1851 on the Shadrach rendition, George Ticknor Curtis was, in the parlance of the abolitionists, the "slave law commissioner", a role he also played to a judgment in the Sims rendition two months later. His role earned him several stripes in the Parker Trial, such as:[27]

It was Mr. George T. Curtis, the only brother of the honorable Justice now on the bench, — born of the same mother and father, — who had the glory of kidnapping Mr. Sims; it was he who seized Shadrach, and gave such witness against one of the Angels of the Deliverance, and then came back and enlarged his testimony; it was he who declared the rescue an act of "treason;"…

---

[25] Parker Trial 169, 218–219.

[26] *E.g.*, George Ticknor Curtis, *A Treatise on the Rights and Duties of Merchant Seamen, According to the General Maritime Law, and the Statutes of the United States* (Boston 1841); *id.*, *A Treatise on the Law of Copyright, in Books, Dramatic and Musical Compositions, Letters and Other Manuscripts, Engravings and Sculpture, as Enacted and Administered in England and America* (London and Boston 1847); *id.*, *Commentaries on the Jurisdiction, Practice and Peculiar Jurisprudence of the Courts of the United States* (Philadelphia 1854). Curtis's career is bracketed by the publication of his *Digest of Cases Adjudicated in the Courts of Admiralty of the United States, and in the High Court of Admiralty in England* (Boston 1839) and his successful appeal for a Mormon convicted of bigamy in *In re Snow,* 120 U.S. 274 (1887). There appears to be very little biographical material about this Curtis, who seems to have rivaled his better known brother in legal ability and output.

[27] At 6.

DRED SCOTT V. SANDFORD

In the Curtis Memoir, the tangled history of the adjudication of the *Dred Scott* case is laid out in detail by George Ticknor Curtis.[28] An action brought by Dred Scott, claimed as Sanford's slave, for his own freedom and freedom for his family, it came to the Supreme Court on a brief factual record that the parties had stipulated in the United States circuit court for the district of Missouri. In the lower court, Sanford first sought dismissal of the action by a plea in abatement on the grounds that, as Dred Scott was black and his ancestors had been slaves brought from Africa, he could not be a citizen of the State of Missouri, and therefore could not invoke the diversity jurisdiction of a federal court as provided in the Constitution. The circuit court overruled this application for dismissal, but on the merits it found that prior owners' having taken Scott and his wife temporarily into Illinois or territory where slavery was prohibited by the Missouri Compromise did not make them free when they returned to Missouri.

The case was first argued in the December 1855 term of the Supreme Court on both the jurisdictional question and the merits. Initially the Court, over the dissents of Justices Curtis and McLean, intended to avoid the jurisdictional question and sustain the decision of the circuit court on the merits by applying Missouri law, which did not recognize *de jure* emancipation from such temporary sojourns. However, the Court ordered reargument of the case at the December 1856 term on two additional questions it framed on its ability to consider facts concerning Scott's slave status alleged in the

---

[28] Curtis Memoir, Vol. 1, 192–242. An even fuller presentation appears in George Ticknor Curtis, *Constitutional History of the United States from Their Declaration of Independence to the Close of Their Civil War* (2 vols. New York 1889 and 1896) (hereafter "Curtis Constitutional History"), Vol. 2, 266–278. See also, Don E. Fehrenbacher, *The Dred Scott Case: Its Significance in American Law and Politics* (Oxford 1978). "Sandford," used in the caption, is a misspelling of "Sanford," the actual name of the claimant.

initial jurisdictional pleadings in the circuit court. On March 7, 1857, in an opinion by Chief Justice Taney joined by Justice Wayne, and with separate concurrences from all the other justices save McLean and Curtis, who filed separate dissents, the Court ruled that blacks could not be citizens of the United States, that the Constitution and the Judiciary Act granted blacks — whether slaves or free — no rights of any kind, including the right to sue in federal courts, and that Congress had exceeded its Constitutional powers in the barring slavery in the territories in the Missouri Compromise of 1820.

Justice Curtis's dissent joined issue vehemently on both aspects of the Chief Justice's opinion. Recent scholarship with regard to the citizenship issue asserts:

> Even if constitutionally sound, the Curtis position "was hardly a triumph of antislavery ideology." For all practical purposes, Curtis denied citizenship to all persons of color not born in New England. His celebrated dissent on citizenship was based entirely on a technicality. *** Had Sanford claimed when challenging federal jurisdiction that Dred Scott was not an American citizen, Curtis would have voted with the *Dred Scott* majority. [29]

Much more compelling for this analysis is the other ground asserted by the Chief Justice's opinion: that the Missouri Compromise of 1820 was unconstitutional.

As mentioned earlier, George Ticknor Curtis was one of the counsel for Dred Scott. According to his *Constitutional History of the United States*, after the case was set down for reargument on the two additional questions, Montgomery Blair, representing Scott:

> requested me to aid him two or three days before the case was called. I replied that on the question whether a free negro could be a "citizen," there was not time for me to make the necessary preparation, but that on the question of

---

[29] Mark A. Graber, *Dred Scott and the Problem of Constitutional Evil* (Cambridge 2006), 56.

the power of Congress to prohibit slavery in a territory I thought I could be of use even on so short a notice. It was agreed between us that I should argue the latter question, and that Mr. Blair should argue the former one.[30]

Two or three days was all Curtis needed to prepare an oral argument which fills a 40-page pamphlet.[31]

Acording to George Ticknor Curtis's later writings on *Dred Scott*:

> After this second argument, and at some time during the same term, Mr. Justice Wayne became convinced that it was practicable for the Supreme Court of the United States to quiet all agitation on the question of slavery in the Territories, by affirming that Congress had no constitutional power to prohibit its introduction.[32]***

> Judge Wayne made strenuous exertions to convince the chief-justice that if a majority of the court should decide these questions as he (Wayne) wished them to be decided, all further agitation on the subject would be quieted, and therefore that for public reasons this should be the disposition of the case. It was in vain that Justices McLean, Nelson and Curtis, in the conferences of the court, explained in the strongest terms that such a result, instead of putting an end to the agitation in the North, would only increase it, and that the influence of the court, its estimation in the country, and its true dignity rendered it most inadvisable to have it understood that the decision of these very grave and serious constitutional questions had been influenced by considerations of expediency.[33]

---

[30] Curtis, *Constitutional History* at 272–273 n.1.

[31] *Argument of George T. Curtis, Esq., in the Case of Dred Scott, Plaintiff in Error vs. John F. A. Sandford, Delivered in the Supreme Court of the United States, December 18, 1856.* It is is a subject upon which he published more than once. George Ticknor Curtis, *The Just Supremacy of Congress over the Territories* (Boston 1859).

[32] Curtis Memoir Vol. 1, 206.

[33] Curtis Constitutional History at 274–275.

Although crediting Justice Curtis with the stronger position on the merits, scholars have weighed in on the reasons for the intensity of his dissatisfaction with the Court's handling of the *Dred Scott* case. [34] Maltz even criticizes Justice Curtis's assertion that Taney's treatment of the Missouri Compromise was *obiter* as the product of his "intent on striking back at Taney and the other Southern Justices" for addressing that issue and the result of judgment "distorted by the heat of the controversy" to "reach[] for an untenable argument to discredit Taney":

> When his political beliefs were strongly engaged, even a judge as committed to legal ideology as Curtis was willing to twist doctrine in order to vindicate those beliefs. [35]

As noted earlier, the Missouri Compromise was bitter medicine for Joseph Story and those who shared his views. In return for letting Missouri join the union as a slave state, rather than contain slavery where it was, the North received the offsetting admission of Maine as a free state, but also a territorial limitation on slavery thereafter. While that limitation had recently been relaxed by the Kansas-Nebraska legislation in 1854, there had never been a suggestion that any such restriction of slavery was constitutionally prohibited. As a result:

> Wherever it was believed that the Supreme Court had lent its weighty authority to the doctrine that the restriction against slavery was unconstitutional, a storm burst forth. [36]

Six months later, after a bitter correspondence with Chief Justice Taney over the latter's refusal to allow Justice Curtis a copy of his opinion, Justice Curtis resigned from the Supreme

---

[34] Richard H. Leach, "Benjamin Robbins Curtis: Judicial Misfit," *The New England Quarterly* (1952), Vol. 25, 507; Earl M. Maltz, "The Last Angry Man: Benjamin Robbins Curtis and the *Dred Scott* case," 82 *Chi.Kent L. Rev.* 265 (2007).

[35] *Id.* at 276.

[36] Curtis Constitutional History at 277.

Court on September 1, 1857, although he appears to have made up his mind no later than July. This correspondence, and what is known of the circumstances of his resignation, are provided in the Curtis Memoir by his brother, George Ticknor Curtis. According to the Memoir, apart from financial considerations, Justice Curtis's resignation was prompted by the *Dred Scott* case:

> [I]t was a conviction, more or less justified by what occurred before the adjournment of the court, but held with entire sincerity, that he could no longer expect, on constitutional questions, to see the court act with that judicial propriety and consistency, and that freedom from political considerations, which alone enable it to retain the confidence of the country.[37]

Thus, it wasn't about the slave: there is nothing about Curtis's stance that suggests that his dissent was in any way influenced by the consequences of the *Dred Scott* decision for Dred Scott or other slaves.[38] His battle, as his brother's had been at the reargument, was for the balance of national political power between North and South under the Constitution, just as it had been Story's in 1820, and the result was his conviction that the Supreme Court majority was tampering with it based on the sectional interests of a majority of the justices. Albeit on the losing side, in a way Justice Curtis's contest with Chief Justice Taney in *Dred Scott* was the same, *mutatis mutandis,* as Chief Justice Taney's with Justice Story in *Prigg*, not to mention Story's subsequent proposal to Senator Berrien, devastatingly summed up by Finkelman:

> In the end, then, *Prigg* was an opportunity to expand federal jurisdiction that Story could not pass up. The cost of

---

[37] Curtis Memoir, Vol. 1, 211–232, 243–244, 249–250, 258.

[38] Graber, *supra*, page 99, n. 29, at 77–78 asserts that, before and after his Supreme Court tenure, Curtis was a "white supremacist" who "consistently adopted anti-egalitarian, racist positions," and that his dissent in *Dred Scott* was an exception.

that gain was the freedom of some free blacks and fugitive slaves. But, it was a cost Story was willing to pay since it was paid by people like Margaret Morgan and her children.[39]

THE APOTHEOSIS OF JOHN CAPHART

With the outbreak of the Civil War John Caphart, Shadrach's pursuer, reinvented himself as a jailor at Castle Thunder in Richmond, a military dungeon for 400–500 Confederate soldiers awaiting court martial, "disloyal persons" and "Yankee prisoners." For several days in April, 1863, a committee of the House of Representatives of the Confederate States conducted hearings about the conditions there. Caphart was one of the witnesses, testifying to his decades of experience in corrections work prior to his arrival in 1862 at Castle Thunder, where he thought the treatment of prisoners was "very favorable" compared to other prisons: "[N]ever saw prisoners better treated." Other warders saw severe whippings, shootings, death from exposure and "bucking" — defined as "to tie the arms at the elbows to a cross-piece beneath the thighs." One of the warders testified that Caphart was "very abusive" to prisoners, another that Caphart was inhumane and gratified at a prisoner's "chastisement," and a third that Caphart had carried out orders to whip eight men on a single occasion, although he did allow that "the prisoners...threw bones at Caphart because they hated him generally." Another testified:

By the Chairman:

Question: You know Caphart?

---

[39] Paul Finkelman, "*Prigg v. Pennsylvania:* Understanding Justice Story's Proslavery Nationalism," *Journal of Supreme Court History* (1997), Vol. 2, 51, 61–62. *Ibid.,* "Joseph Story and the Problem of Slavery: A New Englander's Nationalist Dilemma," *Massachusetts Legal History* (2002), Vol. 8, 65.

Answer: Yes, sir; I do.

Question: What is his general disposition; is he kind?

Answer: He is exactly the reverse of that.

Question: Did you ever hear him express any regrets for punishment inflicted upon soldiers?

Answer: No, sir; he rather exulted at it. I have heard him say, "Damn them, I'd take a knife and cut them to pieces."

An Englishman arrested as a spy testified:

Question: What is the general character of Caphart? Is he kind?

Answer: I would say not; rather brutal; I have known instances where he has been ordered to tie up and buck prisoners and he seemed to take a special pleasure in it. He would tie them up as tight as possible.

In their report of May 1, 1863, a majority of the five-man committee recommended that no action be taken by the House, praising the fitness of the administration of the prison and the importance of prompt and rigid discipline. The other two members of the committee denounced the corporal punishments inflicted as illegal and barbarous, one noting that: "Firmness and promptness are very different from torture and inhumanity."[40]

---

[40] *The War of the Rebellion: A Compilation of the Official Records of the Union and Confederate Armies*, Series II, Volume V (GPO 1899), 871–924.

CHAPTER VI

Conclusion

One of the most celebrated statements in American jurisprudence appears at the beginning of Justice Oliver Wendell Holmes's dissent in the *Northern Securities* case:

> Great cases like hard cases make bad law. For great cases are called great, not by reason of their real importance in shaping the law of the future, but because of some accident of immediate overwhelming interest which appeals to the feelings and distorts the judgment. These immediate interests exercise a kind of hydraulic pressure which makes what previously was clear doubtful, and before which even well settled principles of law will bend.[1]

The "hydraulic pressure" of presiding at a trial, intent on enforcing the Fugitive Slave Act in the face of a local widespread popular movement implacably opposed to it, led Justice Curtis to make rulings and give jury instructions inconsistent with existing authority and practice and detrimental to the defense at the *Morris* trial.

Following the Rescue cases he had no occasion to address the authority of the jury. His opinion in *Morris*, departing from what had been the clear rule at the founding of the Republic on the role of the jury in criminal cases, has created uncertainty on a central Constitutional issue still not finally resolved by the Supreme Court of the United States, which, in 1895, expressly adopted Justice Curtis's exposition of the law, including his misreading of *Brailsford*, discussed above.[2]

---

[1] *Northern Securities v. United States*, 193 U.S. 197, 400–401 (1904).
[2] *Sparf and Hansen v. United States*, 156 U.S. 51, 64–65 (1895).

In contrast to a softening of some of the other positions he took at the *Morris* trial, Justice Curtis stuck to this one. At Wright's first trial, the defendant asked to argue to the jury its power to judge the law, citing one of the favorable cases which had eluded John P. Hale and Richard Henry Dana, Jr., at earlier trials.[3] But Justice Curtis refused:

> The Judge said he could not hear any further remarks on that point, that the decisions of this Court upon it have been such that it must be considered as settled, unless the Supreme Court of the United States should reverse it. Such a reversal he considered very unlikely to be made, as he was acquainted with the opinions of all the Judges of that Court except one, and they agree with his own. He was acquainted with the case which Mr. Wright wished to cite. He had examined the subject very fully, reflected much on it, and was very clear about the correctness of the view he holds.[4]

Several years later, Justice Curtis reiterated the same view in correspondence with his uncle, George Ticknor:

> Mr. Hale had a quarrel of a violent character with the Supreme Court of New Hampshire, some years ago on this subject of the right of the jury to judge the law. He was entirely worsted. He renewed the contest before me in the Circuit Court with no success. *** It is the opinion of every judge save one, now on the bench of this court, that, under the Constitution of the United States, the jurors are never judges of the law. I say save one, and I do not know what his opinion is.[5]

Justice Curtis's views in *Morris,* as adopted in *Sparf and Hansen,* remain the black letter rule in the courts of the United States. In relatively recent times, the United States Court of Appeals for the Second Circuit has had several

---

[3] *State v. Croteau*, 23 Vermont Rep. 14 (1849).

[4] *The Commonwealth,* June 10, 1852.

[5] See, *supra,* pp. 86–87, n. 10. Justice Curtis was referring to the *Small* and *Pierce* cases, discussed above at pages 20–21.

occasions to revisit the doctrine and has adhered to it zealously.[6] That said, the doctrinal position is eroding in two respects.

First of all, some district judges support now a jury's ability and even their own — "to say 'no' to official power when that small word must be uttered for the sake of freedom…, to make the law make sense, to temper the law's iron logic with fairness, moderation and mercy…"[7] In *Pabon-Cruz*, to prevent a district judge's potential triggering of nullification by informing the jury of the mandatory 10-year sentence on conviction, the Second Circuit was forced to issue a mid-trial mandamus. A recent study of the jury by a group of sociologists criticizes the position since *Sparf and Hansen* this way:

> In other words, juries retained their right to independence but lost the right to be *informed* of that authority. This paradoxical state of affairs has resulted in the occasional

---

[6] *United States v. Carr*, 424 F.3d 213 (2d Cir. 2005), cert. denied, 546 U.S. 1221 (2006); *United States v. Pabon-Cruz*, 391 F. 3d 86 (2d Cir. 2004); *United States v. Thomas*, 116 F.3d 606 (2d Cir. 1997). *Thomas* involved the district court's discharge of a juror, during deliberations, "for refusing to convict "because of preconceived, fixed, cultural, economic, [or] social…reasons that are totally improper and impermissible.'"

[7] William L. Dwyer, *In the Hands of the People: The Trial Jury's Origins, Triumphs, Troubles, and Future in American Democracy* (New York 2002), xiii, 62–63. Although getting the underlying procedural history of the Shadrach Rescue cases egregiously wrong ("Eight of his rescuers – four black men and four white – were indicted and placed on trial in Boston. *** In the first three cases enough jurors held out for acquittal to prevent a verdict from being reached. Discouraged, the government dropped the remaining cases."), Judge Dwyer speaks approvingly of the Rescue cases as trials at which "many jurors answered the call of conscience." *Id.* at 74. He takes a distinction between a jury's "law-defining" and its acquittal "on grounds of conscience"; for purposes of this paper, they are the same.

jury defying what they consider as unjust applications of the law.[8]

More recently there has been a far more direct and protracted confrontation between a district judge and the Court of Appeals.[9] And earlier, in one celebrated case just prior to *Thomas*, a district judge, sitting without a jury at a trial at which he should never allowed himself to preside, claimed this right for himself as the trier of fact in acquitting two Roman Catholic clerics of criminal contempt for blocking the entrance to an abortion clinic in defiance of an earlier permanent injunction against them.[10] Judge Sprizzo first asked rhetorically:

> Were a person to have violated a court order directing the return of a runaway slave when *Dred Scott* was the law, would a genuinely held belief that a slave was a human person and not an article of property be a matter the Court could not consider in deciding whether that person was guilty of a criminal contempt charge?

In the end, however, the answer to that question was not dispositive:

> However, even assuming arguendo that the Court were satisfied that the Government's proof established the requisite wilfullness, the Court would still find the defendants not guilty. The facts presented here both by sworn testimony and a videotape depicting an elderly bishop and a young monk quietly praying in the Clinic's

[8] J. Gastil et al., *The Jury and Democracy: How Jury Deliberation Promotes Civic Engagement and Political Participation* (Oxford 2010), 93.
[9] *United States v. Polouizzi*, 549 F.Supp.2d 308 (E.D.N.Y. 2008), vacated, 564 F.3d 142 (2d Cir. 2009), on remand, 687 F.Supp. 2d 133 (E.D.N.Y.), rev'd, 393 Fed. Appx. 784 (2d Cir. September 22, 2010). The *Pabon-Cruz* and *Polouizzi* cases both involved possession of child pornography.
[10] *United States v. Lynch*, 104 F.3d 357 (2d Cir. 1996), cert. denied, 520 U.S. 1170 (1997).

driveway, clearly call for what Judge Friendly once referred to, in *United States v. Barash*, 365 F.2d 395, 403 (2d Cir. 1966), as the exercise of the prerogative of leniency which a fact-finder has to refuse to convict a defendants, even if the circumstances would otherwise be sufficient to convict. *But cf. Sparf and Hansen v. United States*, 156 U.S. 51 (1895)(outlawing practice of permitting counsel to argue to jury that it could return a verdict contrary to law)[footnote omitted].[11]

A divided panel of the Second Circuit dismissed the Government's appeal for lack of jurisdiction,[12] and rehearing *in banc* was denied by an equally divided full court.[13]

Second, *Thomas* was decided without the benefit of the Supreme Court's decision in *Apprendi v. New Jersey*, 530 U.S. 466, 498 (2000), which, it has been suggested, may signal a return to an express acknowledgment of the jury's role beyond simply factfinding.[14] Subsequent authority has strengthened his prediction. In his dissent in *Sparf and Hansen*, Justice Gray made the following observation:

> But, upon the question of the true meaning and effect of the Constitution of the United States in this respect, opinions expressed more than a generation after the adoption of the Constitution have far less weight than the almost unanimous voice of earlier and nearly contemporaneous judicial declarations and practical usage. ***But the question what are the rights, in this respect of persons accused of crime, and of juries summoned and empanelled to try them, under the Constitution of the United States, is not a question to be decided according to what the court

---

[11] *United States v. Lynch and Moscinski*, 952 F.Supp. 167, 170 n.3, 171 (S.D.N.Y. 1997).

[12] *Id.*, 162 F.3d 732 (2d Cir. 1998).

[13] 181 F.3d 330 (2d Cir. 1999).

[14] Jenny E. Carroll, "The Jury's Second Coming", 100 Georgetown L. Rev. 657 (2011); Donald M. Middlebrooks, "Reviving Thomas Jefferson's Jury: *Sparf and Hansen v. United States* Reconsidered," *American Journal of Legal History* (2004), Vol. 46, 353, 415. Judge Middlebrooks outdoes Rev. Theodore Parker in his treatment of Justice Curtis.

may think would be the wisest and best system to be established by the people or by the legislature, but what, in the light of the previous law, and of contemporaneous or early construction of the Constitution, the people did affirm and establish by that instrument.[15]

More recently, a divided Supreme Court, requiring jury consideration of sentence-enhancing misconduct, concluded:

> Ultimately, our decision cannot turn on whether or to what degree trial by jury impairs the efficiency or fairness of criminal justice. One can certainly argue that both these values would be better served by leaving justice entirely in the hands of professionals; many nations of the world, particularly those following civil-law traditions, take just that course. There is not one shred of doubt, however, about the Framers' paradigm for criminal justice: not the civil-law ideal of administrative perfection, but the common-law ideal of limited state power accomplished by strict division of authority between judge and jury.[16]

The issue remains one of immediate public interest.[17]

---

[15] *Sparf and Hansen,* supra, 156 U.S. at 169.

[16] *Blakely v. Washington,* 542 U.S. 296, 313 (2004).

[17] Paul Butler, "Jurors Need to Know That They Can Say No," *New York Times,* December 21, 2011, A39. A parallel issue involving the grand jury has divided the judges of the Ninth Circuit. *United States v. Navarro-Vargas,* 408 F.3d 1184 (en banc 2005); *United States v. Marcucci,* 299 F.3d 1156 (2002).

APPENDIX

Justice Curtis's Charge in the *Morris* Case
from the Dana Papers

Preliminary qu. is to powers of Ct. & Jury
Jury must take the law as given by the Ct., and the Jury solely
to apply the Cts [missing word] to the facts

No. [of] substantive charges ag. dft.

1. That S. was held as a slave by DB, that S. escaped to
Mass.—that C. was agent & made complaint, & ct issued
warrant, S. arrested on warrant, held on the order of the court,
made escape, & Dft aided—

2. Riley held S. in custody under process, & Dft obstructed

Burden of proof is on Govt beyond a reasonable doubt—
Defines reasonable doubt—throughout

Charge 1st—no dispute that a man (S. or M.) was arrested,
Caphart had power from De Bree, held under an order, &
escaped by violence

Was S. a slave of DeB. Under the law of Virginia
Was he the same person

Must prove this
(Reads the ev. of DeB & Caphart)

Crit. here is this test[imony] does act to prima facie ev.

[Reads from opinion of Sup. Ct. in 6 Pet. 632 Kelly v. Jackson]

Concl. of the fact, it is, it is decisive.

Jury to try the credit of the witnesses

"If uncontrolled, the duty of the jury is to render their verdict in acc. with it"

Rules and pr. of law as to the cred. of witnesses. (1) Jury to believe a witness unless impeached. (2) may be impeached by evidence of gen.. repute, by [illeg. word] improb. of the story; & his disclosed character, "tempestuous sensibilities."

If not believe Caphart, cannot convict on the first 13 counts. Was Riley "lawfully assisting them"? He was "lawfully &c" as a matter of law.

Did Deft. aid, knowing & willfully assist conspiracy? Not material. Was rescued by people acting in concert. Must have been a concert of interest. When was it formed? How long was it in a state of formation?

(1)   Deft's acts before adjournment
(2)   "   "   after adjournment

As to S's saying "if I die &c," Govt must satisfy jury M's conversation to S. was relating to the rescue. Not enough to show it may be so.

Reads from Judge McLean's charge in 3 McLean 536 Vaughan v. Williams & als. [1]

---

[1] This was a civil action by a slaveholder whose slaves were rescued by the defendant and others after the slaveholder had found and arrested them in Indiana. The portion of Justice McLean's jury instructions that Justice Curtis is likely to have read appears at page 537 of the report:

If he "sanctioned it in any form" he is liable—although he did no act & said nothing – if he gave the information as to who was in ct room, <u>for the purpose of aiding</u> &c —he is guilty. His doing nothing to prevent it, & his pleasure at it, goes to remove the presumption arising from his character. "Good time" or "chance" —directed to take the most favorable phrase to the defendant.

Rule of law as to positive testimony & negative. This is not a case of positive & negative testimony. It is a question as to who the man was.

Under second set of counts not necessary to prove the facts of slavery, attorney &c—

If court made the order, & Riley held S. under the order, he was executing legal process

Same acts which showed aiding under 13 counts, will show obstr. under 3 last counts

Return a gen. verdict of guilty of both or neither. If not so, then spec. no. ct. of each.

It seems that the defendant, Owen Williams, from shortly after the arrest up to the time of the escape of the colored persons, took an active agency in the movements of the company. He did not drive the wagon in which the fugitives were conveyed, nor is there any evidence that by word or action he contributed to the rescue, at the time it took place. But if he countenanced and encouraged from time to time, the movements of the crowd which resulted in the rescue, or being present, sanctioned it in any form, he is liable to the above penalty. A man cannot incite others to the commission of an illegal act, and escape the consequences by the plea, that he did not put forth his hand in the consummation of the act.

Justice Curtis's Charge in the *Wright* Case
from the Dana Papers

October 26, 1852

U. States v. Elizur Wright

A jury must be impartial. As no means of ascertaining the opinions of a jury until they are called, either party and the court may ascertain the impartiality of the jury. May do it even after trial commenced. Propriety of this is demonstrated by the fact that jurors have to [illeg. word] as to be excused—

Interruption of the D. was not because his remarks were not pertinent or proper but because in misdemeanors, <u>closing</u> counsel does it.

<u>Reads Act 1790</u>—If officer has a legal order, any person who interferes by intimidation or act of violence is guilty. Need not prove that Sh. was a slave or a fugitive &c

Wright's state of mind. If at the [illeg. word] and in the Ct room Wright only stated opinions and state of mind, - not relevant. But, if indicated an <u>intent to act</u> in a certain way; & if so they only show that he <u>probably would,</u> not that he <u>did,</u> violate the law.

Govt. says his decl.

If W. made the dec. with intent to intim. the officers with a view to a rescue & had its effect in fact

Prove (1) Did he make them
(2) Did it for the purpose of of intimidation, [illeg. word] to a rescue

Exc. (3) need not prove of an actual plan of a rescue at the time

(4) W's remarks must contribute to the rescue

Beyond a reasonable doubt—

No evidence that the officers were in fact intimidated by W. or that it had any effect

1. Was W outside the green door?
2. Did he there say "in!" "in !"

Clark is a material witness. If he was under control of the Govt., and not produced, the Govt. having the burden of proof, the presumptions are ag. the Govt.:

Rules of experience as to judging of facts—

1. If direct confl. ev of cred witnesses, must try to reconcile it.
2. Dft. presumed innocent, & satisfied beyond a reasonable doubt—defines "a doubt for which a sound reason can be given"—
3. If cannot so reconcile evidence so as to remove reasonable doubts, is not guilty.

Act 1850 Co. the same, except it must be proved that Sh. Was a sl. By the law of Va—

Rules of ev for this case are the rules of the Comm. Law, not the rules of Va. The presumption of the Comm. Law is that all men are free—

Being held and treated as a slave is ev. of slavery, but does not constitute slavery.

[What are the facts to be proved? Must not the facts which constitute the status of slavery?

INDEX